To
Cousin Bob
Hope you Enjoy
Mike

Life in a Blue Suit and Different Coloured Neckers

Written by Mike Screech
Illustrated by Pam Screech

Published by Lyvit Publishing, Cornwall

www.lyvit.com

ISBN 978-1-914206-02-3

Life in a
Blue Suit
and Different
Coloured Neckers

Introduction

This book is quite unusual as it has been written, first of all, over fifty two years and, secondly, it is about life in the Royal Navy and the Scouting Association. There have been, as you can imagine, lots of lapses of concentration and for that matter a certain lack of interest. I sent it to a Writer at a School of writing. He told me that the amount of bad language in it was unacceptable, so I have toned this down. I have had to change a lot the names in this book for two reasons. First of all, to protect the occasional innocent and, secondly, so that I can't get sued.

The book is written based on a lot of fact and a little fiction. I cannot tell you which bits are false because a lot of the stories have been told me by some wonderful shipmates who I felt obliged to believe. My original inspiration was reading the book The Red Sailor by Patrick O' Hara in 1903.

Thanks must go to all my old Shipmates, some of them are mentioned here, some obviously not. Scouters, who have been many, but mostly I suppose my West Taunton friends, Ann, Jaquie, Bob, Dave Twigger, Jim Neal. Last but not least, my wife Edwina and my children, Deana, Paul and Russell, and their children and also their children's children, who they have kindly lent me from time to time. Also thanks to my late Mum and Dad, my brother Roger, and my eldest late sister Ann who encouraged me to write this. My sister Pam, who has done all the illustrations in this book, and Rita our baby sister, who is always constant. All of these people deserve my thanks and apologies for putting up with my strange nautical and scouting ways.

Anyway, God forgive you all.

As a side note...

Just to explain a bit about this book and tell you what you,
dear reader, have got to understand, is that although it is
not all true, most of it is. I have left out some of the juicer
bits on purpose. However, most importantly, it is to show
you in some small way that from the age of seventeen until
I was about twenty two, I had to put up with a lot of
bullying in my Naval career. Some of it went on until I was
nearly forty years old, mostly by officers and gentlemen
who should know better. That is why in my scouting life I
can and will not put up with boys and girls being bullied.
Unfortunately there are Senior Scouters that think it's very
clever to bully leaders. You know who you are so God Bless
and forgive you. I can't!

Chapter One

How it Began

I have to start with scouting, as this is where I started. Like most boys in my day, at eight I joined the Wolf Cubs. It was at a pack called St Josephs 3rd Waltham Cross in Hertfordshire, which seemed to be miles from my home in Ponders End, Enfield. I've got say here that I loved being a Wolf Cub. We played a lot of games that are actually banned today. I stayed on when we were invited to join the Scouts. I sort of liked it, especially the camping bits and going to Gillwell Park, and Tolmers Scout camp. However, I was also keen to join the Navy, so at thirteen decided to join the Sea Cadets. My Dad wouldn't let me belong to both, so I decided that I would be a Sea Cadet at T.S. Eagle in Ponders End. I can't say I enjoyed it much, there was a lot of bullshit, so at fourteen I decided to join another local Scout Group. I did this and joined St George's Enfield, I think it was 13th Enfield. This was attached to St George's Catholic School.

I was fifteen when I left school and, although I didn't leave the Scouts, I wasn't so active. I did various jobs which included being a trainee motor cycle engineer, a shoe shop assistant, and a page boy in a Hotel in Piccadilly. When I got to five foot four inches I was told I was too tall for that role, so they told me I could try to be a porter but I would have to carry cases that could be the same size as me. Instead I went back to work in W.B. Williams shoe shop. I applied to go into the Royal Navy twice during this period, the first time I was refused as I had eczema on my hands. On the second attempt I didn't think my chances were very good, I told my boss Mr Alan that I wasn't very well and went for another attempt at Holborn recruiting Office. Unfortunately one of the girls, Doreen the supervisor at the shop, told Mr Alan where I had really gone and, when I went back the next day, he sacked me. I had been accepted by the Navy, so I asked around the shops if anyone had a job for me. The owners of the local fish and chip shop gave me a job until I received my call up papers.

I had made a friend at the recruiting office called John Brand and we envisaged joining up together. We hung around with each other on John's Lambretta Scooter. I was having a great time until John got his call up. He was going to HMS Raleigh to be a seaman. Since I was joining as a Steward I wasn't called until two weeks later, so I was told to join Raleigh on the 7th June, 1964. When I was in my New Entry training I had a visit from John, who was already two weeks into his training. Unfortunately that is the last time I ever saw him. I don't know if he finished training or not and I still try to this day to get in touch with him, but to no avail.

I managed to get through the first six weeks of my training, but was feeling pretty homesick. Don't get me wrong, I did enjoy it, apart from the boxing bit where I was put in to box against my class leader, Eric Presley, who happened to be a junior champion of Devon. He did not go easy on me at all and decided that he would show the class and instructors why he was a champion. He pummelled me.

In our last week of training we had to have meetings with the Padre. As a Catholic, myself and Eric had to have a meeting with the Catholic Priest who was asking if we were happy and enjoying our new life. I told him that I missed my scouting. He suggested that I join the Deep Sea Scouts. A few days later he said that I had been accepted into the D.S.S. and gave me some badges for my shoulder and a leather band with the scout sign in brass for my wrist. I also got a blue neckerchief and a badge to sew on the back of it. There was another boy in training who belonged to the Plymouth Scout Group at the Cathedral. The priest invited us to a Wolf Cub meeting at the Catholic Cathedral in Plymouth to help out. I enjoyed it so much that I felt sure that scouting would be another important part of my life, and so it was.

Once my part one training had finished, my class and I were going to our part two training. Most of us were going to Chatham in Kent to become Cooks, Stewards, Stores Accountants and Writers. The rest of the class were going onto other training, mostly to the Fleet Air Arm camps in Cornwall and Scotland. Eight of us were joining the Stewards School under Petty Officer Steward Trevor Levy.

We were initially put in an accommodation block on the top floor. There were already three other classes in the mess and each one was a week further ahead than the next. A class leader was allocated and our class leader was Eric Presley. We also had a Mess leader who was the class leader from the most senior group. This man was called Dan McGovern, a Scouse who looked as hard as nails. He started his introduction by trying to bully all us younger boys, but he didn't realise that our class leader Eric would not stand for any bullying, so he was very apprehensive about shouting at us when Eric was around.

After settling in, P.O. Levy had a chat with us and told us that he played rugby for the Combined Services Club in Gillingham, and that if any of us would like to join him then he would be happy to put us forward. I was only five feet five at this time and I told the P.O. that I was not interested in playing rugby, but did he know of any Cub packs in the area that I may be able to help with. His wife was a Cub Leader at a pack in Gillingham and she was glad of the help, so I helped out at this pack for a few weeks on a Wednesday evening. I loved it and I was given a fair amount of responsibility, which was nice as, during the day, I was just a number.

Our part two training consisted of waiting at tables, valeting officers' uniforms, cleaning officers' cabins and public rooms, cleaning silver, polishing glasses and other menial tasks for the officers. We were also taught bar work, including looking after beers, learning cocktails, and learning wines of the world and how to keep them. I enjoyed this part of the training more than anything else.

I started to learn a lot of disrespect for the officers, some of whom were not much older than us and were basically snobs who talked down to us at all times. At this time I did not drink any alcohol at all, and I couldn't understand why the blokes over twenty years old got so worked up about getting a tot of rum and water every day, and to be honest it stunk. I learnt differently when I became old enough. We were also issued with three white waiter jackets with enough white buttons for one of them; they were so uncomfortable and did up right to the neck. They had royal blue collars and cuffs. We were also issued with white gloves, only to be used when serving at tables. We were only given two pairs of these. I don't know how quickly most people lost theirs but mine lasted three months maximum.

Part of the course was to do a week's sea training. Ours was supposed to be on HMS Defender, but it was cancelled. The reason given was that it had broken down, but it was very suspicious that the Chief Petty Officers and Petty Officers were having a Summer Ball and all the trainee classes were expected to work towards that and the officers Summer Ball. We spent the week moving furniture, putting up decorations, cleaning silver cutlery and table decorations in both messes. The day before we were taught how to make up various salads and were then allocated which mess we would be working in on the day of the balls. I was allocated the Chief and P.O.s mess, as were all P.O. Levy's favourites. I was glad because I had decided that I did not like the officers very much, rather strange as I had joined as an officers' steward.

I must say at this point I didn't want to join as a steward at all, my Dad told me that I wouldn't be allowed to join if I went as a cook, which is what I wanted. He said, "No son of mine is going to be a slosher." On the night of the ball we were all inspected in our relevant messes and then given a briefing of how it all worked. We were all supposed to lay the plates down at the same time, they helped themselves to the meat and salads, and then when the Maître D' lifted his hands we all had to start clearing away the plates. We then lay sweet plates all together when we

9

were instructed to do so. It was actually good fun, and it was all quite impressive.

After the meal we were given silver salvers and told to stand in the bar area, and when we were called to a table they would order drinks from us. We would then go to the bar, order the drinks, get the bill, and serve the drinks before collecting the money from whomever ordered them. This was great. We discovered right from the off that they would tip us, too. We soon learnt the tables that were the best tippers, and it wasn't the tables that had our instructors on, so they were avoided like the plague.

At about two in the morning we had to give out coffee and biscuits, carriages they called it. Then about four a.m. we had to start clearing away, finishing any washing up that needed doing. We were then sent away to go to bed and reminded that we had to be ready to march to the parade ground at nine in the morning. This was regarded as a lay in from the instructors, the majority of whom did not turn up for the parade, though it still went ahead. As I said before, I didn't drink in those days, but there were plenty of the Stewards that did and some of them had drunk a fair bit in both of the messes.

The Stewards that worked in the Officers Mess were very jealous of us because they got no tips at all, but they did have a lot to drink, they were told by the Leading Steward that was one of the perks of being a bar steward. Anyway, after the parade we were told where we would be going on draft a week later after a very long weekend at home. In our spare time the next week we had to pack our kit bags and any cases we had to get ready for our next move. On the Wednesday I went to cubs and they presented me with a book written by Baden Powell called Scouting for Boys. It was very good of them and I was quite sad to be going.

There was a lad from Yorkshire called Dick Pratt and he intended to stay at Chatham as it was too far for him to go up North for the weekend since he was joining a ship in Chatham the following week. However, the Navy said that he could not stay in barracks and that he would have to go somewhere. He was in a bit of a quandary as he didn't have a lot of money. The Navy would give him a travel warrant to go home, but he didn't want the embarrassment of going home with no money. The other problem for Dick was that he had given his civilian clothing away and wouldn't be able to buy any more. I phoned my Mum and told her the situation, to which she told me to bring him home and he could borrow some of my clothes. So that's what we did.

Dick was impressed with London and all the trendy people. I lent him some of my clothes, but they were all too small for him really. He also had to wear the underwear we had been issued with and it itched like mad. I threw mine away that weekend, apart from the couple of things we had to keep for kit musters. But I would never don those horrible things again.

On the Tuesday both Dick and I had to go back to Chatham to pick up our first ships. When we arrived at the dockyard we told them which ships we were joining. They phoned Dick's ship and a Jeep was sent to the gate to pick him up. We said our last goodbyes and I never heard from Dick again. One of the dockyard policemen came over to me and said, "I'm sorry son, but your ship's not here, it has apparently broken down in Londonderry, Northern Ireland. You will have to go into the Regulating Office in HMS Pembroke and await further instructions."

Off I went, carrying my heavy kit bag and holdall the half a mile to the regulating office. After waiting for someone to see me for ages, finally P.O. Levy came in and said, "Hello son, have you got problems?" I explained to him what had happened and he took charge of the situation. He got one of the regulating leading hands to look up what I should be doing. My orders were to go to London, then get a sleeper train to Scotland, where I was to get a Ferry across to Belfast, then get a train to Londonderry, where I would be picked up and taken to my new home. He issued me with different warrants for my journeys, then P.O. Levy organised for a van to take me to the station.

I was on my way, my uniform was looking quite untidy, and I wasn't feeling very clean by the time I got to London. I was really quite sweaty carrying all that stuff. On the sleeper train to Scotland, I didn't sleep really as I was worried I may miss my stop and it was very noisy all the time, but it was in the age of steam trains, so I suppose it would be really. I got my train from Belfast to Londonderry and I arrived on the Wednesday, mid-morning. I had very little money when I got to Londonderry so I couldn't afford a taxi, instead I thought I had better wait until the Navy sent transport for me. Eventually a Naval Jeep came and I asked him if he was there for me. "Don't know anything about you, Fella", he said, "What you here for, anyway?" I told him I was there to join HMS Hardy in the dockyard. He told me he was there to pick up an officer who was going to HMS Sea Eagle, the shore base. He would ask him if he could take me to the Dockyard first.

When the officer emerged from the station, the driver told him my situation. He told me to get in the Jeep. When we were driving along, the officer told me that he would take me to Sea Eagle as the Hardy was not in. I arrived at the naval base and the driver took me to the regulating office. They were very kind to me; the regulators were Northern Irish guys. "We will get you a bed here for the night, and sort you out in the morning", they said.

The next day I went to the regulating office and the leading regulator said, "Well mate, you won't be going to the Hardy for a while as she is somewhere at sea, but apart from it being in the Irish sea somewhere we don't know where it is. You can't work in the officers mess as they are all civvies, so you can work in the junior rates mess. If you want to go ashore you're allowed to wear civilian clothes, and if you want to go across the border you will have to wear civilian clothes." I explained that I was not allowed to bring civvies as I was joining a ship, straight out of training. "Well, make sure you don't go over the border then, or you won't be allowed back in."

I got paid that day and issued with my cigarette tokens. I was owed quite a lot of money. That lunchtime the cooks were going to the local pub and were putting some bets on and watching the horse racing on the pub telly. They invited me along, I still wasn't drinking but I decided I would like to go and thanked them. One of them was about thirty and was telling me that he had four children, and things were tight. He then asked me if I could lend him fifty quid. He promised that he would be able to get it back to me the next day. Well I lent him the money, and needless to say I have never seen it again. I wasn't used to people like that.

The following morning I was sent to the regulating office, where they told me that the Hardy would be in Chatham in two weeks, so they would make arrangements for me to go there. I thought, that's another pay day, so the leading cook who I lent the money to would pay me back. Pay day came and went, and I kept myself to myself. I gave my cigarette coupons to one of the seamen that worked in the dining room, for which he seemed grateful. He told me that the civilian supervisor was actually an IRA Captain. I asked him if that was true and he said that if I told anyone he would have me killed.

My day came and I was driven to the station, I had said my goodbyes and was promised that my fifty quid would be sent on to the Hardy. The IRA Captain told me not to forget what would happen if I told anyone about him. All in all I was pleased to get out of there really. I wasn't issued with a warrant for overnight accommodation, so I was to take my chances on even getting a seat. I did the crossing from Belfast and got on a train from Scotland to London. From there I got a train to Chatham, it felt like going home.

The Navy had a van waiting at the station in Chatham, not for me I might add, but they were willing to take me to the dockyard. There were about four other young sailors in this van, who were all going to HMS Pembroke. They dropped me off at the dockyard still carrying my heavy kitbag and a holdall. I reported to the Police on the gate, and once more they told me that the Hardy had left Chatham that morning. So I had to go back to the regulating office to see what was going to happen to me then. After a while they told me that the Hardy was heading for Bristol, and that is where I had to go. Once again I was given a travel warrant, and transport was organised for a lift to Chatham station. They had been in touch with the ship and had arranged for transport to pick me up there, I would be at Bristol by that evening. So off I went again to join this elusive ship.

Chapter Two

My First Ship

A minibus from the Royal Naval Reserves Bristol picked me up at the station and the civilian who was driving it wished me luck and told me he was visiting the ship the next day. I stood at the bottom of the gangway and had a good look at the ship. I thought that it looked great, but nothing like any of the ships I had seen in Chatham dockyard, or Navy Days at Plymouth. All of a sudden, someone shouted at me from the ship, "Come on lad, get your stuff on board, people are waiting for you." I threw my kitbag over my shoulder, carried my holdall in my left hand and started my way up to my new home.

As I got to the top this man with an anchor and three stripes on his arm shouted, "When you cross the bow of my ship, you salute, do you understand?" I said that I would have a problem with that as my hands were full. "That's your problem, lad, take one of your bags back off the ship and bring them on one at a time, and make sure you salute each time you come on, is that understood?" As I tried to turn around my kit bag fell off my shoulder and it went onto the jetty. "Leave that there and bring your holdall on board, but don't forget to salute." I did this and, after being told to salute properly and go back and do it again, my salute was acceptable. "You must be the new junior assistant steward. Right, go back to the jetty, get your kit bag, put it on your left shoulder, and come back up again and salute." I struggled to get the kit bag onto my left shoulder, and once again made my way back up the gangway. I saluted the very best I could, and the miserable bloke on the ship said, "Is that your bag, left on my ship?"

"Yes" I replied.

"Don't ever do that again", he said.

He introduced himself as Ginger, the most senior leading hand on the ship, and told me that whenever he is on the gangway he would expect me to bring him a cup of tea or coffee, and to make sure I collected his mug first as the officers wouldn't be happy with me bringing their posh cups to a junior rating. He then made an announcement on the ships tannoy for Leading Steward Bright to come to the gangway. He turned to me and said, "You won't like this bloke, he is a nasty piece of work."

All of a sudden this sailor wearing a white front, with an anchor on his arm, came up to me. He had a very red face and fair hair. He picked up my holdall and told me to follow him. We went past the galley (kitchen) and straight to the top of a hatch. He then threw my holdall down the hatch, and told me to throw my kitbag down. I did this, then followed him and my bags down. There was a door on the right which was an office, and two people were working in there, even though it was 7.30 in the evening. On the opposite side was another door, which is where we went in. Inside immediately on the right was a rack, with what looked like hammocks, and in front of me was a table with three chairs and four bunks. Two men were sitting on the bottom bunks playing cards.

The leading steward, who was called Bright, told me that one of the men sitting there was called Paddy Connell and he was the Captain's leading steward, and the other was a cook called Neville Cabbot, who was the cook's mate in the Wardroom. They both nodded to me and I said hello. The Captain's man said, "Have you brought a hammock with you?"

"No", I replied.

"Well, you will need one as the four bunks are used by the leading hands in the mess which is four and you other five have to sling hammocks. Leading Steward Bright then said, "Get a clean white front out of your bag, put it on, and get up to the Wardroom, you are duty steward today and for

19

the next two weeks as I have had to cover for you while you have been swanning round England and Ireland. I will get the duty stores man to get your hammock for you." I managed to find a cleanish white front from my holdall, but my shoes were filthy. Shiner said, "Don't worry about your shoes, just get up there."

I went up the ladder to the Wardroom, which was just above the mess. The table was laid up in the dining room, the silver was nowhere as clean as I had been used to, and there were six places laid for a three course meal. Shiner then said, "You can call me Shiner when there are no officers or senior rates around, when they are you call me Leading Steward". He also told me that when I had served dinner and cleared up, I should check the room every hour until midnight to see if there was anything the officers wanted. In the morning I was to go back up and lay up for breakfast, then make a big pot of tea, and at seven, start to shake the officers whose cabins were on the next deck up. "I am going ashore now, and I will see you in the morning at about eight, you will then meet the P.O. Steward."

So there I was, on my own, not knowing where anything was, who anyone was and quite honestly shattered. The cook's mate, Neville, came to the tiny Wardroom galley and explained to me what was being served for dinner. He then gave me a briefing on the officers who would be in for dinner and explained about who was who in the mess with roughly what to expect. He told me that he was eighteen and had been in the Navy for a year, he came from Kent.

He also warned me about Shiner Bright, and his boss, the leading cook, who could also be not a nice bloke. He told me that P.O. Steward was the boss, his name was Ted Bennet and he was a good bloke, he said that he would not let me do every duty for two weeks. Only two officers came in for dinner, one was called Sub Lt Preece. He seemed very nice and asked me a lot of questions about myself and where I came from. Another officer came into dinner and sat opposite the Sub Lt. He introduced himself as Lt Cdr King who was on loan from the Australian Navy. He was a very abrupt man, and after introducing himself he told me that whilst he was eating, I should tidy up the newspapers, straighten up the cushions and not to make any noise.

When the two of them had finished the Aussie said that I was to get him a glass of brandy. He wrote a chit of paper with his order on it and slammed it down on the serving hatch. I didn't know where the brandy was kept and told the officer this. He then shouted, "Don't they teach you anything at Pembroke nowadays?" He then showed me where the alcohol was kept and helped himself. I cleared away everything, asked if I could go and went down to sort out my hammock and put my kit away. He told me not to come back that night, but I was not allowed to go ashore as I was duty and may have been called at any time by any officer that may come back before midnight.

I made my way back to the mess and there was someone asleep on one of the bunks, the lights were all turned out, and as I found my way around the mess, found my kit bag had been shoved in a corner next to the sleeper. I pulled it out and over to where my locker was. The sleeping figure then woke up and shouted, "What the fuck are you doing? I'm trying to sleep." I apologised and tried my best to be as quite as possible. Next I found a hammock that had been left just outside the door. I didn't have a clue what to do with it, but I attempted to put it up. It was very difficult as there were three other hammocks already hanging around the mess. In the end I decided that I was not going to succeed, so I laid it out on the mess table. I managed to get it open enough to get into it. Sometime in the middle of the night, I was suddenly rolled over onto the deck (floor) and a very drunk man said, "Who do you think you are? The table is my bed when we are in harbour. Find yourself somewhere else to sleep." I decided that I would just put it under the table, but every so often someone would come in and kick me whilst they were getting into their bunks or hammocks.

I hadn't asked anyone for a call the next morning, so when Neville woke me up at 0645, I rather panicked. I got dressed; I didn't wash as I didn't know where the bathroom was. I ran up to the officers mess and found it locked. Neville told me I had to draw the key from the gangway and, by the time I got back to the Wardroom, it was 0655 and I had to get the tea made and start shaking the Officers in five minutes. Luckily there was a boiler in the pantry and I managed to get to the first officer's cabin within seven minutes. I knocked on the first Lts door and heard him say, "Yes?"

I told him it was the duty steward for his morning call. He told me to enter. I asked if he wanted a cup of tea. He answered that he did with two sugars, and pointed to where his cup was. Then he asked me my name and why I was late. I went and took tea to the other officers cabins. There were only four officers in their cabins. Once the shakes were done, I rushed down to the Wardroom to lay up for breakfast.

When I arrived in the mess there was an officer sitting in the lounge part, he was setting out some newspapers on the benches and asked me why I hadn't done that already, and why there was no table laid up. I quickly laid up and asked him what he would like, I told Neville what he wanted, put some toast in the toaster and got the officer the cup of tea that he asked for. Before long the mess had five officers sitting at the table, I took all their orders and took them to Neville. Each of the officers introduced themselves to me and I was quite pleased that they all got what they had ordered. Leading Steward Conoll came to the Wardroom Pantry and asked me if I was okay.

In the next few minutes Shiner Bright, the P.O. Steward and the leading cook all came up to the pantry. The P.O. introduced himself as Ted, had a little chat with me, and asked if I had been on my own. I told him that I had as I was duty steward. He then shouted at Shiner and said, "What do you think you were doing? You should have done dinner and breakfast and given young Mick a chance to settle in."

Shiner was not happy. He turned to me and said, "Go down to the mess, have your breakfast, and sort your hammock out, and I want you back here at 1200. Also report to the Coxswain, so he knows you have arrived." In the Coxswains office there was another person who also had an anchor on his left arm, which indicated he was a leading hand, but on his right sleeve was a crown, which indicated that he was a patrolman (policeman). He seemed a nice guy and gave me a card to take to different people on board to stamp so they would have then known I was now one of the Ships Company, and the caterers would know they could claim for another mouth to feed. I believe they were given £1. 18 shillings a day to feed me. I then had to sign for my hammock and all the ropes to go on it, also for my mattress and pillow, my plates, knives, forks and spoons etc.

I managed to sort everything out with half an hour to spare. I made my way to the Wardroom. Ted the P.O. was standing in the passageway having a cigarette. "Are you okay young Screechy?"

"Yes, thank you", I replied.

"Well, you have got to go and have a joining interview with the boss. Follow me." I followed him up the ladder to the Supply Officers cabin. Ted introduced me to the Lt. who then introduced himself and told me he was not really a Supply Officer, but a Seaman Officer, who did the divisional officers role for the stewards, cooks, stores accountants and writers. He then asked me how I thought I would like it on the ship. I told him that I didn't like being a steward, and that my ambition would be to become a leading patrolman, like my father. He told me that I would need to get to be a leading steward first, and to grow a few inches. If I really didn't like being a steward I could think of something else and he would try to sort it out for me. I enjoyed my conversation with him, and told him about the run around I'd had, and how I was treated on my first day on the ship. He was very sympathetic and told me he would be having words with all concerned. I then realised it was a mistake to have given him all the information. He did have words with all concerned, and I was then treated fairly badly by all concerned, including Shiner Bright, who then decided to treat me twice as badly as anyone else.

The Sunday afternoon came and the ship was suddenly full of people who had gone home for the weekend. In the Wardroom we suddenly had ten officers for tea and dinner and I was kept very busy, making and serving tea and cakes that Neville had made. At dinner all of the officers came into dinner in their posh clothes, with bow ties and dinner jackets or civilian clothing. The leading cook was on duty with Neville and steaks to order were one of the choices for the main course. Most of the officers had soup to start, whilst they waited for their steaks to be cooked. Lt Cdr King asked for a blue steak, which I had never heard of before. I told the leading cook what had been ordered, and I said that Lt Cdr King had ordered a blue steak, and I laughed. All of a sudden a knife came flying through the hatch between the galley and pantry and stuck in a cupboard door, just missing my head. The leading cook then suddenly rushed through to the pantry, grabbed hold of me by the neck and shouted into my face, "Don't take the piss out of me, or Lt Cdr King, if he wants a blue steak then that's what he will have, and you had better learn how it is done because there will be times when you will have to do it yourself, do you understand, sprog?" It shook me up for the rest of the meal; in fact it made me wish I had never joined.

The officers were given a savoury course after the main, then they had dessert after that, where they had a plate with a brass finger bowl on it with just a little water, and a small knife and fork also on the plate. When they had finished that they then ordered a small coffee. They then sat at the table chatting for ages, drinking port and brandy and whatever else they fancied. I had to hang around all evening to clear up and wash up when they had finished. I really did not like those officers from then on. I knew that as soon as I could, I'd get out of that ship, in fact out of the steward branch as soon as was possible.

I then had the difficulty of getting into my moving bed. To be honest it was the most difficult thing I had ever attempted. All the others seemed to look easy and open, but mine was closed up on each end and every time I thought I would get in, I fell out of the other side. One of the cooks who I kept hitting when I fell then showed me that I needed some cut up broom sticks to shove between the nettles (strings). This then opened it all up.

The next day, Shiner and I were both on duty for every meal, every day whilst at sea. We also had to clean the officers cabins, the passageways, the bathroom and toilets. We also had to clean the junior ratings toilets and bathrooms. Of course, because Shiner was a leading steward, he was not expected to clean any toilets or bathrooms so it was down to me. Whilst I was cleaning the officers toilets I felt the urge to have a pee. I shut the door and someone tried to get in. When I had finished I came out to be confronted by a Lt. He said "Have you got ideas of grandeur young man? Now go and report yourself to the coxswain, and tell him that you have illegally urinated in an improper place, namely the officers heads."

I reported to the coxswain, expecting him to laugh about it, but he didn't. In fact, he wrote on a charge sheet what I had done. He told me that I would be on the officer of the day's defaulters later that day. I was called to the Captain's flat (passage) at 2pm. I was marched to a small table, where I faced the same officer who caught me. I was ordered to "off caps" and the charge was read out by the coxswain. The officer then said, "You have been found guilty as charged and you will do three days number nine punishment." Afterwards the Coxswain told me that I would have extra work to do for the next three days, which was an extra four hours a day, in whichever department they would tell me at the times allocated. Also if the ship had to call into any port I would not be allowed to go ashore in that period.

The ship then headed up the Irish Sea. We were exercising in the Irish Sea with a submarine, the sea was really rough, it made working in the officers mess rather difficult since things were being thrown about, including the furniture. Ted then told us to tie the furniture up and make sure everything was stowed away. The mess looked very untidy and any officer that came in for a coffee soon took it to their cabins or place of work as there was nowhere to sit. Most of the crew were sea sick and a lot took to their bunks and hammocks. Ted then told me that the following night we were going into defence watches, and that meant that we were all to do four hours on and four hours off.

As far as the catering staff were concerned we had to be available during these watches on a four hour basis in our own departments. If an officer required anything during that time we had to get it for them. It also meant that during the night we had to take it in turns to take KY round the whole ship. Ted took me and Neville to the main galley to show us how to make it. Pots and pans were moving around the galley and water was all over the deck (floor), it was very dangerous just trying to get around. We had to get a big fanny (pot), put in a big bar of chocolate, two pounds of sugar and four tins of carnation milk. Then we had to put this fanny under a steam pipe and mix the ingredients up. Finally we put the full pot in the sink to catch any spills and ladled the mix into a six pint teapot.

The first person to get the drink was to be the Captain, but we first had to go to his pantry and get out one of his special fluted, bone china cups and a saucer. We then had to carry this pot and cup and saucer to the bridge. This proved to be very difficult as the ship was moving up and down and from side to side. We then had to pour this drink into mugs for everyone who was in the bridge area. All the ratings had their own mugs, but the officers mostly didn't, so they had to go to the Wardroom and get bone china cups for themselves. You could only imagine how many of those cups survived.

Anyway, I thought I was very lucky as I was allocated the first KY watch between 2000 and 2359. I struggled but managed to get the drink ready, went to the Captain's pantry and got his fluted cup and saucer out. I then made my way up to the bridge, I really struggled to get up the ladder but, as I got to the top, someone came in from the bridge wing and, as he opened the door, so came a massive goffer (wave). It hit me and knocked the Captain's cup and saucer out of my hand, crashing to the deck; it also knocked the pot out of my hand. Everyone on the bridge was shouting at me and someone said, "You bloody little idiot, now you had better start again." So that's what I did.

The next attempt was more successful and everyone on the bridge got their KY. I then had to make my way outside to go to the wheelhouse behind the bridge. There were eight levers on the door that I had to undo whilst keeping hold of the pot. I eventually got inside. Standing, leaning on the wheel was the miserable Leading Seaman Ginge. Sitting on the deck was a young seaman. I poured their KY into their mugs. Ginge said, "Look, young Screechy, if you have to come here again I will let you steer the ship if you want." That sounded exciting so I looked forward to doing my next shift. I then had to go back to the galley and re-heat the remainder of the KY. I made my way on the open deck to the engine and boiler rooms. To my horror, there were what seemed to be lots of straight ladders going down. A Chief Petty Officer came alongside me and said, "Don't you try and get down there carrying that son; I will get the lads to come up and collect their own." This they did, much to my relief. The chief told me that I was not allowed down there as you had to have overalls on. So that was my first KY watch and I was looking forward to getting in my hammock for the rest of the night.

At 2330 I had to wake up the next person to carry out the KY watch. Neville was the one I had to call. I found his hammock in the dark and woke him up. He then told me he was feeling ill, asking if I'd do his watch for him. I agreed to do it for him, went back to the galley and prepared to carry on doing the next shift.

I made the KY, went to get the Captain's cup and saucer and made my way to the bridge. The sea was a lot calmer then and getting to the bridge was not so difficult. However, when I got to the bridge the Captain was not there. Lt. Cdr King was now in charge of the ship. He told me that he would have the Captain's cup as he didn't have one of his own. I didn't see any harm in this, and poured him a cup of KY. Another officer was there with him and asked me to go to the Wardroom to get him a cup as he didn't have one. I did this, but to my horror when I got to the Wardroom pantry, there were cups smashed all over the floor.

I managed to find an unbroken one and took it back to the bridge. Lt Cdr King then told me that when I had finished taking the KY around I would need to come back and collect all the officers cups from the bridge take them back to the

Wardroom and wash them up. I carried out the rest of the KY watch without incident. I went back to the bridge and collected the cups and some saucers, those that weren't broken, took them back to the Wardroom and washed them. I then cleared up the pantry of all the broken crockery. There were only four unbroken cups left. I thought, well, that's not my problem; little was I to know!

At 0330 I went back to my mess to wake up the next person. He was a cook who was in his thirties and a very miserable person. When I woke him he told me that he had been very ill all night and that I would have to do his watch as well. I told him that I was very tired and wanted to get to bed. At that the horrible leading cook leaned over from his bunk and said, "You just get on and do it, Screech. We will sort this out with Ted in the morning, understand, boy?" So it was I had to do it all over again. At 0600 I had to clean up the main galley as part of my punishment. Then I had to get the breakfast for the mess and take it down to the cooks and stewards. Before I could eat mine, I had to stow away my hammock as it was in the way. Everyone was moaning at me again and I wished I wasn't there anymore.

At 0800 I had to go back to the Wardroom. Outside was the leading cook who was called Tony, along with Shiner, Neville, Paddy and Ted. They were standing round smoking. Ted then turned to me and said, "Do you know what an S126 is, Screechy?" I replied that I did, it is a charge someone has to pay if they lose or break something. "Well, you're going to get a big one", said Shiner.

"You're getting one off me aswell", said Paddy.

Ted then told me that the cups and saucers that were broken the previous night and the Captain's cups that were broken were my responsibility. I tried my best to explain that none of these were my responsibility as they were left on the bridge, and officers were helping themselves to them, and I had seen it happening all night as I was the only one to do all the KY watches. My pleas were wasted and Ted gave me a form to sign to say that I owed £12.00 - that was more than double my weekly wage. I really felt that everyone was against me.

At the end of our exercise we were heading back to Londonderry, which was the ships home port, the ship being part of the Ulster squadron. My punishment was also completed, so I was hoping that I might be able to go ashore and maybe find a Scout group that I could go and help out at. The first problem I found with this task was that, as a junior rank in the British Navy, we had to go ashore in our uniform. The officers had to go ashore in civilian clothing while the Senior NCOs could go ashore in uniform but they were allowed to go to some changing rooms in the dockyard and change into civilian clothes. Most of the people locally avoided the people in uniform.

Since I didn't drink at all still, there was nowhere for me to go except for a visit to the people in HMS Sea Eagle. I called into the pub where the crew from Sea Eagle used to go. There were several people from the base in the pub and they invited me to join them and have a drink. I eventually accepted a pint of beer (my first), and I quite enjoyed it. One thing led to another and I enjoyed a few more. They told me that they were going to a place in the town, just an ordinary house. One of the lads told me it was called "Ellen's Glop Shop". It was interesting as all that was sold was a flask full of a red wine that they called Glop. This was very pleasant and very strong. When it was time to go I was very drunk.

We then got a taxi to the Diamonds Bar. I was warned that this pub's main customers were IRA people and the guy from the camp who was IRA would probably be there. Because I was in uniform I got some terrible looks. After this we were going across the border. We got into a taxi and was warned that when we got to the border I would have to get down and hide so they couldn't see my uniform. I did as I was told, and as we reached the border I hid down.

We reached a pub just inside the border and got out of the taxi. I was told to hide my hat under my Burberry (raincoat) and stay in the background. As we walked into the pub, one of the bar boys (fourteen years old) noticed I was in uniform and shouted out, "British Sailor, we don't want no trouble in here", which bought attention to myself and all the customers turned to look. When one of the sailors went to the bar, an older man behind the bar said, "You can only have one here then I'll be asking you to leave." As we were leaving the customers turned to watch us leave and started to boo us. Luckily the taxi was waiting and he rushed us back to Derry.

The next night I was duty, we sailed to carry out fishery protection off of Scotland and the only incident we had before going into port was when the Captain made a pipe (tannoy broadcast) to tell us that we were going to help out a boat in the Irish sea. It turned out to be an RAF boat and it was letting water. I went on deck with Neville to watch, and one of the Petty Officer Seamen told us that we would get extra money for saving this vessel. Of course that was more baloney from another so called expert.

Once we had towed the RAF launch into Faslane in Scotland, we went on to Wick and then Nairn in the Scottish highlands. It was really beautiful to see, but no-one stayed ashore after about 2000. A lot of the crew went fishing off the stern and I spent a few hours watching proper fish being pulled in while people were asking the cooks if they would cook the fish for them. The cooks were doing it with the promise of sippers, gulpers, half tots and even full tots of rum. Some of the cooks such as Neville were too young to have the rum but would do it for cigarette coupons.

After Nairn we headed for Rothesay, we were going to be there for three days and three nights. The same rules applied we had to go ashore in uniform as did everyone, except the officers. I went ashore at about 1700 and had a little wander around, I found a little shop, bought a pie, and asked the lady if she knew of any scout groups in Rothesay. She told me that she ran a cub pack that evening. She invited me to stay for tea and to help out with the cubs, then two hours later to help with the scouts. That was great and my run ashore sorted. I had a great evening, finding it hard to understand the accents but they did scouting things the same as everyone else. I loved it, and when I finished I promised I would go back whenever I went into Rothesay again.

After Scouts was finished and we had cleared up, two of the leaders asked me if I would like to go for a wee drink with them. I was happy to go with them. When the pub closed they took me back to the house where they lived and we had a couple more drinks. At 2230 I told them I would have to leave as I only had leave until 2359 as I was still a junior. I got back to the jetty where we were getting a boat back to the ship, only to find I had missed the last one. On the jetty I was the only junior and the other matelots all had leave until 0800. There was a barge alongside that was open, so we all went inside and lay out on the benches and slept. At 0500 we were all rudely awoken by two burly Scotsmen telling us to get off their boat. We did as we were told and went out to the freezing jetty to wait for the ships boat to pick us up. Everyone was taking the mickey out of me for being late. Finally the ships boat came and we all piled on board.

When we arrived at the ship the sea was rough, the ships boat was tossing around and the seamen were finding it hard to get alongside. It had to go away from the ship several times before we were all able to get on board. By the time I got aboard it was 0820. I should have been at work by 0800. I went straight to the Wardroom and Shiner was waiting for me. He was so angry, his face was red and he was shaking. He said to me, "The Wardroom has to be cleaned throughout, the silver has to be cleaned, the cruets have to be cleaned and filled. The glasses have to be polished, the table polished with vinegar and water, all the furniture has to be dusted, the cabins have to be cleaned, beds made and all the bulkheads drawers and desks have to be cleaned." I replied that I would do it as soon as I got changed. Shiner then plunged at me, grabbing me around the neck and bringing his fist back to hit me. The leading cook, Tony, jumped out of the small galley and grabbed Shiner's arm and held him back. Just then Ted came round the corner and pulled me into the Wardroom. He shut the door told me to sit down and sat opposite me.

He first asked me why I was late for duty. I told him the truth about the lady in the shop, and the cub meeting etc. He obviously thought it was a bit far-fetched and thought something went on between me and the lady, giving me the nods and winks etc. He then told me that I would be in the shit for coming off shore late, and also for turning to (starting work) late. He then told me to go and change into number eights (working clothes), then go to the coxswain's office with my cap. I went to the mess and found that my hammock had been slung for me for the night, but was still

37

up. I had to stow it away before I could do anything else. Paddy then came into the mess and told me to sit down as he wanted a little chat with me. I quickly got into my number eights, and then sat down on one of the bunks. Paddy said to me, "You know you are a double of how I was when I was young steward, always in the shit, always late, and very unpopular with the killicks (leading hands)." He then told me that I needed to sort myself out, and just do as I was told. He would protect me from Shiner, but just do as he told me. At this point I wondered what I could do for the best, I was not a naughty person but everything was pointing to that being the case.

I reported to the coxswain's office where the leading patrolman shook his head and said, "Where are you coming from, young fella?" I just shook my head and said nothing. Then Ted came to the office and told the patrolman that another charge would have to be made against me. I was also late for turning to. The leading patrolman shook his head and said to Ted, "Do you think that's fair, P.O? I certainly don't think it is. If that does go ahead I seriously think that Leading Steward Wright should also have a charge brought against him for what I believe was violent behaviour, don't you agree P.O?" Ted then told him to forget the other charge against me and forget the charge against Shiner.

I was then taken again to the Captain's flat where I waited to be called to the table. "Junior Assistant Screech, right turn, quick march, halt right turn, off caps." The officer of the day found me guilty, but because it was a recurring offence he would have to send me to the First Lt's table. Then it was right turn, quick march, and report to the office.

I went to the coxswain's office, and the coxswain said to me that I would be going to the first Lt's table at 1400, and to make sure I was clean and smart. I then returned to the Wardroom. Shiner was apparently doing the officers' cabins and Ted was polishing the silver in the pantry. He told me to do the glasses and cruets and lay up for lunch. I carried out what I was told and everyone was silent. They all, including the chefs, had a tea break, but I wasn't even offered one.

At 1100 we had to go to our mess and have our own lunch before going back to the Wardroom to serve the officers. There was a terrible atmosphere and no one spoke to me except to say what they wanted to eat and drink. Actually that suited me to the ground; I didn't like anyone except Neville anyway, so it was best not to speak. When the officers had finished eating and had left the mess, we just had to clean up the Wardroom and pantry, prepare for afternoon tea, then have a break. I decided not to go to the mess, but to just go outside and watch the sea going past.

At 1345 I was called to the coxswain's office. There were three of us there, all to go to the first Lts table, all on different charges. We were then marched to the Captains flat. As I was the most junior I had to go before the Jimmy (first Lt) first. I was marched in, had to remove my hat, the charge was read and I was asked if I pleaded guilty or not guilty. My divisional officer told the Jimmy that I wanted to plead guilty. At this the Jimmy said, "Guilty, 14 days number 9s and ten days stoppage of leave. Right turn, quick march, report to the coxswain's office and wait." At the office the punishment I was given was explained to me. I had 14 days of the extra work, which also meant stoppage of leave. The 10 days stoppage of leave would run alongside of the number 9s, so really I had 14 days extra work and 14 days stoppage of leave and that was it. I then vowed to myself that I wouldn't get any more punishment as long as I was in the Navy. I knew that I had been bullied, though, and there was no way I could say that to anyone. For the 14 days I worked doggedly at everything I was told to do. For ten days of it we were at sea anyway, and the only ports we went into were Rosyth naval base, a couple of small anchorages off of Scotland where hardly anyone went ashore. So I didn't lose too much.

The day my punishment finished the ship went into Clydebank. As we tied up alongside the jetty was full of young girls cheering and screaming at all us sailors on board. We were then informed that there was to be a dance ashore to welcome us, only Ships Company and girls were invited. Everyone on the ship was excited except for the officers who were not invited, and everyone had to be in full uniform. This dance was to be held on the Friday evening. Unfortunately I was duty steward so I was not allowed to go as I had to serve the officers' dinners. If Shiner had swapped duty with me I would have been okay, but Shiner, although not going ashore himself, would not do it for me. He said he was a married man and didn't want the temptation. So it was, I had to stay on board, and most of the officers went ashore anyway. There was only one officer for dinner and he wanted to eat early, so I had to spend the evening in our little mess with Shiner as my only company. Still, I didn't have any extra work on so I put up my hammock and all the rest and was in bed by 2130.

The next day, on the Saturday, I asked if anyone was going ashore but, as usual, nobody wanted to go ashore with the youngest crew member who was still too young to go into a pub. I decided that I would go for a walk on my own. I saw a sign for Glasgow and thought I would walk that way as far as I could. Off I went in my uniform and headed for Glasgow. I was about a mile from the ship when I was approached by two men. The first man, who appeared to be drunk, said, "Hey are you a sailor?" It was difficult to understand what he was saying; I had never heard a person with such a broad accent.

I answered him in a hesitant way and said, "Yes I am".

He said, "What football team do you support then?"

Proudly I said, "Spurs".

"Who?" he asked.

"Tottenham Hotspur", I replied.

He then said, "Are they English?"

"Yes", I replied.

"Aye, but which Scottish team do you support?"

After thinking for a couple of minutes I replied, "Celtic."

At that the other man hit me on the chin and I fell to the ground.

The first man then asked again, "So who do you support?"

Once again I thought for a few seconds then replied, "Rangers", as I was getting up.

As I said that the first man then hit me hard on the chin, and once again I fell to the ground. The two men just walked away laughing.

I felt so fed up, I got up and decided to go back to the ship. My cap was missing, my uniform was filthy and I was quite shaken up. A few yards down the road I found my cap in the road, it was all bent where a lorry had run over it. When I got back to the ship, Ted was standing on the brow. He saw me and came rushing down the gangway and helped me back on the ship. I told him what had happened. When on the ship, Ted took me to the Wardroom and got me a cup of tea, he then told me that I should go and wash my clothes and he would press my uniform for me. Only one cook was in the mess and he decided to help me, taking my dirty bits of kit up to my hammock and washing my kit for me. My faith in human nature was restored to an extent.

Later on that day I was sent for to the coxswain's office where two burly policemen were waiting to interview me. I gave them my statement, but of course I never heard anything about it from that day to this.

I decided that I definitely need to get out of this mess I was in, so I sent away for a clarinet from the NAAFI. I decided that I would learn to play it and then I would apply to transfer to the Royal Marines band. When it arrived there was no way that my mess mates would let me practise in the mess, so I went on the upper deck every day with a 'learn to play' book and it was going quite well. I practised every day for anything from an hour to two hours, I loved it and other people seemed to enjoy it, too. I was also promoted to assistant steward when I reached eighteen years of age. I was getting on better with my mess mates, though they still wouldn't go ashore with me. Still, life was a bit better and I used to go ashore to watch the ships football team play.

At long last we were going on my first foreign visit. We were going to Oporto in Portugal, then on to Gibraltar. After that we were going back to the UK, we weren't sure where but probably Chatham, Kent. We had to take on stores before sailing from Devonport. Apart from fresh food, milk and bread, we also had to take on loads of

43

glasses,cups and saucers as the sea was expected to be rough before Oporto and losses were predicted. The glasses were for the officers to have a cocktail party in Portugal, so they had to be stored under the seats in the Wardroom. To be able to do that we had to take all of the spare seat covers out of those spaces. Once they were out and the glasses stowed, we had to change the seat covers, the ones we took off were bundled up and sent ashore for dry cleaning. The ones we put on were quite new and fitted a lot better than the ones we'd taken off. It made the Wardroom look fairly tidy. It was a hard day all together and, after we had served dinner that evening, we were all shattered and ready for bed.

The next morning at silly o' clock, we had to prepare for sea in the Wardroom before shaking the officers. This meant making sure everything was tied up and rubber mats were placed on the surfaces to stop things slipping. Then we had to call the officers and start serving breakfast. Breakfast was very fast as all the officers had to prepare to sail at 0730. It was quite exciting, thinking that in a couple of days I would be in a foreign country for the first time in my life. The sea in the Atlantic was quite calm and everything seemed to be fine, so everyone was relaxed. That was until we reached the Bay of Biscay. The ship was tossing around and, although we had the rubber mats down, things were still being thrown around the place while furniture still moved around. It was a good job we didn't have to do any KY watches.

The next day we arrived in Oporto. The ship was surrounded by small boats, some had young boys diving into the water chasing coins etc. that some of the sailors were throwing into the water for them to bring up. People on the boats were also trying to sell things to the crew, without success. We tied up alongside, then had to prepare an early dinner for the officers before preparing for the cocktail party. A lot of the ships company were going ashore, but there was no leave for any cooks or stewards as we all had to get ready for what Paddy called the cock and arse party. Mind you, the officers couldn't go ashore either. When we were ready for the party we then all had to get into our best uniforms. A couple of men who were on punishment were given the job of washing up in the small pantry. They were not allowed to finish until everything was done. They didn't seem to mind though, which I found strange.

At around 1800 the guests started to arrive, most of whom seemed to be British which surprised me, although there were a few locals as well. We had to stand in the entrance of the Wardroom with a silver salver of drinks. The only drinks on the Salvers were Horse's Necks (brandy and dry ginger), gin and tonics, and whisky. Once all the people had a first drink, Shiner told me to start to serve the horse's duffers. There were cocktail sausages, small bits of cheese on toast, cheese balls and a mixture of other things. Whilst I was doing this Shiner and Paddy were busy serving more drinks whilst Ted was pouring drinks out. Occasionally Ted was pushing drinks into the pantry for the washers up, and some were being passed through to the galley for the cooks.

By 2000 the officers and guests were quite the worst for wear and started to leave the ship with each other. We opened the pantry door to give us easier access to the dirties etc. The two sailors were both drunk as skunks and were really enjoying themselves. The cooks in the galley were also drunk. They'd almost finished anyway, so Ted told them and the washer uppers to go, and said that we would finish up. The cooks and Paddy decided that they were going ashore, as was Ted, so Shiner and myself had to finish everything ourselves. We had to get ready for breakfast lying up. One officer remained sitting in the Wardroom drinking coffee, he was the Officer of the Day, and he had to stay on board.

The next day I was off duty from lunchtime. I asked if anyone wanted to go ashore with me, but as usual I was on my own. Many of the guests from the cocktail party were owners of port vineyards and had invited a lot of the ships company to their yards for a sample of port etc. so that's where most people were going, including officers. I didn't think I should get involved with this so I decided that I would see if there were any scout groups that I could visit. I ended up at a fairground, which was very good. A man and his son came up to me to talk about my being a sailor, they both spoke English well and it turned out the man was married to an English lady. I had a good evening with them and the man paid for everything. He then told me that his son was going to cubs the next day. I explained that I was a scouter and was hoping to help out at a group. He arranged to pick me up at 1830 the next day to introduce me. I would have to get Shiner to do my evening dinner for me, although my cigarette coupons would come in handy for that.

When I got back to the ship at about 2100 I went to the mess and Shiner was reading a book. He said to me, "Are you back for the evening now, Screechy?"

I replied I was.

"You wouldn't like to look after the duty officer for me would you?" he asked.

"Well", I said, "I will if you could do me a favour tomorrow."

"Yes", he said, "That's not a problem as long as you do lunch and afternoon tea first."

So that was it arranged. The night was, needless to say, a very disturbed night as the mess members arrived back on board at all hours. Tony and Paddy were the very worst for wear and decided to turn all the lights on in the mess and sit around drinking tea for what seemed like hours. Shiner came back on his own and was shouting at the other two to be quiet, after which Tony and he started a fight in the mess. They were banging into the hammocks and falling all over the mess, the mess mirror was knocked off the bulkhead (wall) and it smashed. Then they were grabbed hold of by other mess members and, although it got quieter, the lights were left on.

The next morning the lights were still on and the mess was a tip. I got out of my hammock, stowed it away, and went up to get the officers shakes and breakfast ready. I cut my toe on the broken glass, but it wasn't too bad. None of it bothered me as I was looking forward to my evening. I just carried on doing my job for the rest of the day. Ted arrived at 0830 and asked where Shiner was. I told him I didn't know. He went down to our mess and got everyone that was still there out of bed. They all had to come to work, but they were all the worst for wear with cuts, bruises, black eyes and everything you would expect from a mass brawl.

I had to carry on doing most of the work, but it kept me busy. The whole of the mess except for me were in front of the Officer of the Day. They all got a telling off but, as there were no witnesses, that was all they got. However, they were all told they could not go ashore that day as they were all duty. Ted then told me that if I wanted to go ashore for the rest of the day, that would be fine. I got my uniform on and went for a walk around the town after my lunch. I wanted to be out of the way before the mess members had their tots as I had a feeling that something might have happened after that and I wasn't allowed in the mess at tot time.

I walked around for a long time, remembering that I had to be back to be taken to cubs. I went past a bar which had an open front. Inside the bar was one of the younger chiefs from the ship. He was an artificer and he'd had a quick promotion. As I had got past the bar, the chief came out and shouted to me to come back and have a drink with him. I explained that I didn't really drink, so I would give it a miss.

"Don't be so silly", he said, "I bet you would love the Port and there is a lovely young girl serving the drinks in there, she will fancy you".

So it was that I sampled my first glass of port. The young girl behind the bar turned out to be sixteen years old and seven months pregnant. She offered to have sex with me, though for four escudos. I declined, but felt really sorry for her as she told us her hard luck story. Instead, I gave her five escudos as a tip.

After a few glasses of port I was well gone and said, "Look, Chief, I have to go as I have got to get back to the ship and get picked up to go to a cub meeting at 1830".

The chief then said, "1830? You have missed that as its now 1900. Tell you what, we will go over the road and have a couple of glasses of port in the bar that everyone else will be in." So I agreed, and off we went.

We sat on a couple of bar stools and, as I looked around, I saw a lot of our ships company sitting around the bar, but

49

there were a number of other sailors with HM submarine cap tallies (ribbons) on their caps. There was the singing of dirty songs going on and everyone seemed to be in high spirits. Then the singing started to become insults at each other. Eventually a fight started between a submariner and one of our stokers. All of a sudden everyone was fighting each other. The barman shouted that he was going to get the police and ran outside. When the police arrived the chief grabbed me and pushed me behind the empty bar. We got on the floor, the chief passed me a bottle of port and grabbed one for himself. We sat on the floor drinking the port and the police got everyone outside, except us. We watched as the sailors were all lined up outside.

The chief then said, "We will go outside the other way and make a run for it."

We went out of the patio door and down the garden, ending up in another street. We thought we had done a good job and started singing God Save Our Gracious Queen as we were swigging at our bottles of port. Suddenly, from behind, we were grabbed by two big policemen who had guns slung over their shoulders. They marched us a few yards to the Police Station. They couldn't speak English and we couldn't speak Portuguese, so they put us in two cells.

A while later a smart looking police officer wearing a white suit came into my cell. He told me who he was in very good English. He also told me that we had been silly young men, though all I would have to do was to apologise and they would escort me back to the ship.

He explained that he didn't want me to get into trouble as he had a son at University in England and he was about the same age as me. I said in my drunken stupor that I could not apologise. He then went into the next cell and told the Chief that if he did not apologise he would get someone from the British Embassy in Lisbon to come and sort it out. He would also be getting an officer from the ship. I heard the chief then apologise, and he shouted to me to do the same. I wasn't given that choice again, so I started to shout at the police to let me out.

The next thing I knew, one of the officers from the ship was standing in the cell telling me that I was a waste of time and that I was always in trouble. He also told me that the Chief was back on the ship. He then said that if the police didn't let me go, I would have to make my own way to Gibraltar to join the ship, so if I wasn't back on board by

0800 the next day the ship would have gone without me. I asked him who would pay my fare to Gib and he told me that the British Consul would arrange it for me but I would have to pay.

I had no choice; the British Consul came to see me two hours after the ship had sailed. He told me that it was arranged for me to go from Lisbon to Gibraltar and I would be picked up by the Gibraltar police to be taken back to the ship. So that is what happened, I arrived the day before the ship and was taken to the Police Station in Gibraltar to await my ship. They actually looked after me quite well, I only had to go to the cell to sleep and, at one point, a policeman took me for a walk.

The next day the naval patrol came to the police station to pick me up and take me back to the ship. These patrolmen were not nearly as friendly as the police. In fact, we had no conversation at all. The ship was tied up on a berth the other side of the dockyard. I walked up the gangway and was greeted by the Officer of the Day, who'd seen me in Oporto; the coxswain was alongside him, the leading patrolman next to him and Ted next to him, the best greeting I had on that ship.

Of course, that was not going to be the end of the matter. I was quickly ushered to the Coxswain's office where I was told that I would be going in front of the Officer of the Day within the next hour, then immediately to the first Lt's table, then I would be going straight to the Captain's table.

I was also told that there was a strong possibility I would be sent to a detention centre with a chance that I would be discharged dishonourably. I had to clean up and report straight to the Captain's flat. I went to the Mess, escorted by the leading patrolman. Everyone in the Mess had to leave while I got changed and I was not allowed to talk to anyone. My Divisional Officer would expect me in his cabin before the table. He asked me what I had done and how I would plead. I realised that I had not got a leg to stand on, so I would plead guilty. Once again I was informed that I could be discharged dishonourably. I wasn't worried really as I thought at least I would be off that ship, the bullying would stop and I would be going home. However, I knew that my Dad would be ashamed of me and I would need to find a job.

The Officer of the Day was as expected, he asked how I pleaded and, although I said guilty, my Divisional Officer said that I had no plea. This was all bull as I knew I would be before the Jimmy next and then the Captain, so no decision would be taken until then. Then the bullshit really began, the Officer of the Day said First Lts defaulters, the First Lt said Captains defaulters, and so I waited for the Captain. The Captain asked me how I pleaded and I said guilty. He then asked for the Chief Artificer to come to the table.

He explained to the Captain that it was his fault entirely. My Divisional Officer then said some nice things about me and he called for Ted to come forward and explain to the

Captain what I had put up with since joining the ship. He said some really nice things and told the Captain that he felt I had been bullied since joining the ship. After all these nice things were said, I was sent away to wait while the Captain, the other officers and the coxswain discussed me. I was then called back to the Captain's table.

The Captain said that he couldn't let this offence go without punishment; however he said there were unusual circumstances. He told me that I would have to pay the ship back for my airline ticket. He then said that I would go to detention quarters for 28 days, suspended for twelve months. I would also have 14 days number nines. That was it; I had to go back to the coxswains office to have my punishment explained to me. As I went to the coxswain's office there were several men waiting at the bottom of the ladder, they were all congratulating me and patting me on the back. I felt very good, but I wouldn't be able to go ashore in Gib and I wouldn't be going home.

I never saw the Chief again as he was sent on draft to another ship which was in Gibraltar at the same time. Shiner was made the Captain's steward and Paddy was to be the Wardroom leading steward. Tony, the leading cook, was changed to the main galley and the cook from there came to the Wardroom. It felt like a fresh start and Paddy worked twice as hard as Shiner. The atmosphere in the mess still wasn't brilliant but I was treated with a lot more respect.

I did my punishment with no further incidents and, because I didn't have extra work if we were to go into any port, I was quite happy to stand in for Paddy. In fact, I actually stood in for Shiner once looking after the Captain, who was really nice to me. It also helped me to practise on my clarinet.

One evening my Divisional Officer was listening to me practising and asked, "Would you like to transfer to the Royal Marine band? When we are in Chatham I will organise for you to have an interview with the WRN Officer if you would like to put in a request."

I filled out the request form and it was on his cabin desk before he got back himself. True to his word, he organised a branch transfer meeting. The WRN Officer informed me that she didn't think playing the drums would qualify me as I had to be able to play two instruments proficiently. However, she arranged for me to go to Deal in Kent to the music school for an interview. I went there on a Monday and the first thing I was tested on was my drumming. The Sergeant asked me if I could blow a bugle. I told him that I couldn't. The next day I was tested on the clarinet. There were two civilian boys being tested the same day. They were brilliant, and I felt that it was over before it started. As it was, they told me that I didn't play the clarinet well enough.

I returned to the ship very disappointed and vowed that I would not play the clarinet again. I went back to work and, after my punishment was over, Paddy asked if myself and Neville would like to go ashore with him in Chatham. We both said it would be good, but I was short of money. Paddy told me not to worry as we would be getting some money when we got ashore.

We went to the first pub we came across and Paddy seemed to know all the customers in there. We then walked down the hill to a pub I think was called the Eagle. Paddy knew a lot of people in there as well, but one man in particular. He introduced Neville and me to him, and this man kept paying for our drinks. Paddy and he were quite familiar with each other. When the man went to the toilet Paddy said to me, "Put this in your pocket", and he gave me a leatherbound sort of stick with a big weight in the bottom. I asked him what it was and he said it was a brown hatter sorter. He said that when the bloke dropped us off at the dockyard, he would keep him busy while I should lean over the back of the seat and hit him as much as I could whilst Paddy took his wallet. I told Paddy I couldn't do that and he replied, "Just do it, right? When I say so, you and Neville get out of the car and run."

When we had finished our drinks the man then said, "Would you boys like a lift back to the dockyard? You can then come home with me, Paddy." Paddy told him that it would be easier if he could drop us off at Gillingham gate as it was closer to the ship. When we got there I said to Neville, "Quick Nev, let's go", and we got out of the car and ran into the dockyard. I didn't ever see or hear from Paddy again. I don't know what happened and honestly I didn't tell anyone about this incident as I was scared. I kept hold of the weapon for a while as I kept thinking that Paddy would be back and he'd ask for it. I was frightened about whether anything would come of it for a long time. A new leading steward joined the ship, and he went to work for the Captain while Shiner came back to work in the Wardroom. Everyone kept asking about Paddy, and I informed our Divisional Officer what had happened that night, but no one seemed bothered.

Soon afterwards a draft came in for me to join HMS Belfast in Plymouth before a transfer to HMS Bulwark for a year or so in the Far East. I was so glad to be leaving that ship and thought, at last, the bullying would be over. I vowed that I would never let anyone bully me again.

Chapter Three

The Next Step, HMS Belfast and HMS Bulwark

I joined HMS Belfast and there were a lot of sailors joining at the same time. It was explained to us that, although we would be living on the Belfast, we would actually be part of HMS Orion. I believe it was all part of the submarine depot ship, and submarines were tied up to us a lot of the time.

There were about twenty people in the mess and we all had bunks. The Leading Hand of the mess allocated me a bunk and a locker. The bunks were three high and the lockers were a lot bigger than I had been used to. Apparently this was because we had to put civilian clothing in these. There was also a shoe locker each under the bunks. There was a shop on board called Bernard's Naval Tailors. I went there and opened an account so that I could buy some new civilian clothes. After I had spent as much as I could on clothes, I found the NAAFI shop which was very small, but where I could buy any toiletries I needed and where I could get cigarettes in exchange for coupons and cash. The manager also told me that if I wanted any other goods I could open an account with them and get things sent straight to the ship. This also seemed a good idea, so I opened an account and ordered a record player.

The next morning we had to don our white jackets minus gloves and report to the Wardroom. It was a lovely room with about four large tables. It had windows all around and on one side I could see Camels Head married quarters, while on the other was the dockyard with its cranes and machinery. The new stewards joined the already present stewards to clean the tables, the silver and glasses, then lay up for lunch. After we had eaten our own lunches we had to be in the Wardroom by 1155 ready to serve the officers lunch.

Two of the older men were already in the pantry, ready to serve the dishes to us and wash up. We had to stand around the side of the room at ease (legs apart and arms behind our backs), so when an officer sat down on our allocated table we had to go to their left and offer them a menu. Once they ordered we had to go into the pantry and tell the steward there what they wanted. If it was a soup it would be put into a large soup plate, and we would then take it and serve it on the left hand side of the officer. We would carry on serving each officer the same way. If we offered them a glass of water, we poured that out on the right hand side. It was very easy to do and it was over pretty quickly.

When lunch was over we were told that some of us were on the duty watch, and after a half hour break we would have to put on our working clothes and report to the duty Petty Officer who would give us our duties for the rest of the day. Some of the others were on the standby watch and they would be cleaning for the rest of the afternoon. They would then be allowed ashore. The rest of the men were told they were finished for the day and were free to do what they wanted. So that was how things worked out.

The next day we would be off after lunch, the day after standby. It all seemed much more civilised. It was indeed civilised and it was a very different Navy to the one I had experienced up to then.

Things were going well, and my record player had been delivered by the NAAFI. I had been home and picked up my records. Most of them were traditional Jazz records, but some of the young men that lived on board had bought their own records. In the evenings, when most of the older men had gone home to their wives, we would play cards and listen to music. The only people that were left in the mess in the evenings were us livers-in and the occasional older person who was duty, so it was quite a civilised existence.

Sometimes, the men who lived ashore would ask us to stand in for them to do the early shift. We younger men would get a fag coupon for doing this for them, whereas the older men would do it for a half or full tot. It was quite a little black market going on. I had joined another local Scout group in St. Budeaux, so my Wednesday evenings were taken up by helping out with the cubs if I was off duty. My record player was being used most of the time though, so some of the other mess members were a little jealous of us.

One Thursday afternoon one of the Leading Stewards asked me if I was going home at the weekend. I told him I was, and he asked if he could possibly borrow my record player and records for the weekend as he was having a party at his house to celebrate leaving the Navy. He promised me that he would bring it back on the Monday and that he would give me a cigarette coupon, which seemed fair enough. However, on the Monday morning everyone else came back but not Leading Steward Davies, and not my record player or records, nor for that matter my fag coupon. When I asked one of the other leading stewards if they knew where he was, he replied that he had gone on draft to HMS Drake for discharge, so we wouldn't see him again. I tried to find him in the barracks but to no avail. I reported it to the C.P.O. Steward, and he said he would see what he could do, but I had the feeling that nothing would be done, and I was right.

From that day on the atmosphere changed in the mess, and us younger guys refused to cover for the older men any more as we felt we couldn't trust them. I did find out that he had gone to work at the Royal Mail sorting office in Plymouth. He will be pleased to know though that I will never forget him with all his cockiness and Buddy Holly glasses. Yes, old man, you are a thief!

On August the 13th, we who were joining the Bulwark had to march with all our kit over to the ship. It looked massive and I was looking forward to it. We had to stand in our sections on the jetty, then were told which messes we would be in and how to get there. Once we had found our mess, which was underneath the Junior Rates dining hall, we were told which bunks we would be in. There were already several men in the mess and they showed us which were our lockers etc.

We were told to sort our kit and bunks out, then put on our white fronts and bell bottom trousers and report to the Wardroom after lunch. This was to be our home for two years, it was quite exciting and I think there were ninety stewards and about twenty cooks living in our mess. They were the officers' cooks, so we would be working closely with them.

That afternoon we were told which watches we would be in and what shifts we would be on. We were also given our morning places of work. Some were allocated to the Wardroom bar, some in the dining room, some to the aircrew refreshment bar, others to officers cabins, some the Wardroom pantry and plate wash. I was told that I would be working in the senior officers' flat and I would have three Commanders to look after. My duties included valeting those officers clothes, cleaning their cabins and doing any washing they needed by hand.

There was a Chinese laundry on board which would do the washing and ironing of everyone on the ship, to have it back within 24 hours. I was introduced to my Commanders and I had the Senior Engineer Officer, the Senior Electrical Officer and the Senior Dental Officer. The engineer and electrical Officers said they would not expect me to do any of their washing but they did require their shoes to be kept clean. However, the Dental Officer was so different. He wanted me to keep all his clothes clean and pressed by hand, then to dry them in his cabin. He also played polo when we were in harbour and expected me to wash his jodhpurs with his polo shirts and ensure his boots were kept immaculate. He was obviously a very nasty little man, and I would certainly avoid going to him as a dentist.

My work was certainly cut out, having to look after these officers in the mornings. I still had to work in shifts in the Wardroom during meals and afternoon work when on standby or duty. Another problem was a number of the stewards had a liking for drugs; some would bring them onto the ship and take them when they were on shift, especially when they were in the plate wash. Some used to intimidate the other stewards to take pills and, if you didn't, you were made to feel like outsiders.

There was also a certain steward who I'd first met at HMS Pembroke and was the senior class leader. He'd been called McGovern but had since changed his name. He had not changed his attitude to other stewards though, he was still a nasty piece of work. He was a muscular guy, but he often went up to the junior rates dining hall and mince (yes mince) around, chatting up sailors and often getting into scraps as well. We all tried to keep out of his way as much as we could. He seemed very friendly with some of the officers, and the priests and vicars, and also with some of the senior rate stewards. Luckily he worked up in the Officer's Bridge mess on his own, so most of the day we didn't see him. We will just call him David for the time being. He was to become a major person in a lot of our wellbeing on the ship.

We eventually sailed for the Far East at the end of August, and our first port of call would be Gibraltar (I remembered it well from the Hardy). I had made a number of mates on the ship and had some good runs ashore in Gib. I also went back to help with the cubs on Gib when I could, so life at this time didn't seem too bad. I joined the Blue Jacket band, which was a military-type brass band. I was one of the drummers and I loved it. One of the musicians, an airman by trade, played the trombone, but he told me he also played the guitar and had just started a group on board if I'd be interested in joining as a drummer. I accepted the offer and went to one of the aircrew briefing rooms that evening to be introduced to another guitarist, another fleet air arm person, and also the leader of the group who was a helicopter pilot. He was the bass player and a lieutenant. I had borrowed a couple of drums from the band room and I seemed to fit in quite well with the others. They liked playing Beatles music and most modern stuff at the time.

We discussed what we would call the group, eventually agreeing on Four Jacks (sailors) and a Knave (naval officer). We rehearsed every evening, mostly after about 8pm when we had finished our jobs, and looked out for a singer to make our number up to four jacks. A leading writer on the ship came for an audition, as well as one or two others, and we chose him as our singer. His name was Tim and he fitted in really well. He could also play the trumpet if we ever needed that.

One evening, Jeff, our leader, took some shirts to rehearsal which had been made by the Chinese tailor. They were great as they had laces in the front, and on each of our pockets we had an ace card. Jeff had a joker on his pocket. We also had to perform in front of the ship's company to decide who would be the ship's official band. There was another group on board who were called the Missing Lynx. They were a band made up of stokers. They were also very good, and they had a brilliant singer, but their music was a bit heavy for most of the ship's company and we were voted as the official ship's band.

Our journey then took us to the Suez Canal. This was a very interesting part of the trip. Most people went to the flight deck to watch our progress which was very interesting. By this time we were in our tropical clothing, and at sea we would wear sandals and shorts during the day. The flight deck was so hot that our feet burned through our sandals.

A group of Arabic men were invited onto the ship. They took all sorts of items for sale and we were invited to barter with them for the various goods. To me, most of it looked rubbish so I didn't bother. People who bought large products such as stools and carpets were invited to label their items and store them in the officers' baggage store, so we stewards then had to stow them away safely. The Gully Gully men (the Arabic men) were then escorted off the ship. They gave the Captain and the Master-at-Arms presents and left.

Our next port of call was to be Aden. We were allowed ashore but we had to stay in groups of at least six. We were warned that we should stay together, and not be tempted to go with locals who offered us cheap cameras, watches or the like. We were told that they would lead us into traps, where we would be kidnapped or killed. There were soldiers with weapons all along the route to town who warned us all the way. Those of us in our group found our way into a bar. Outside several young men invited us to come round the corner to buy cheap stuff. We were also offered girls, or boys, for sex. However, we all stuck to our plan of having a few drinks and then got back to the ship.

Over the road from the bar was a Hotel which looked fairly posh. A couple of the group said we should go to this Hotel which was officially out of bounds to ratings since only officers were allowed to go there. We went with the majority and made our way to the Hotel. However, we were stopped outside by a few soldiers who would not let us in. Suddenly, there was an explosion from across the road at the bar we had just left. There were still a few British sailors in there. We were all shocked and made our way quickly back to the ship. We decided there and then that we wouldn't go ashore there again.

Although we had a couple of calls, including Labuan and Guan, we were looking forward to our arrival in Singapore more than anything else. We were going into Singapore in procedure Alpha (ceremonial entry). As a drummer in the band I had to be on the Flight deck, so someone else had to do my morning job.

I was standing on the right hand side of the band at the front as we were heading past Malaysia, a shot rang out and it hit my drum. The band carried on playing as no one had heard the shot except me, and I'd felt it hit my drum. In my innocence and ignorance I thought perhaps it was normal here. It wasn't until we were going back down to the band room that I mentioned it to the band sergeant.

"Why didn't you say something?" he said.

I replied that I thought everyone had seen it and heard it. He immediately took my drum and made his way to the bridge to see the Captain. A short while after we had docked the police came onboard and an announcement was made that an incident had happened on our way in. I was sent to the regulating office where I was questioned by the police, but I had never heard any more about it, and I was simply given a different drum.

An electrician on the ship advertised a drum kit for sale. I went to see it and bought it from him for £100. I had to pay him in stages but he was happy with that. It was the best drum kit I ever had; it was a yellow colour, and Jeff got a card made up for the front of the bass drum with four jacks and a Knave on it. They let me keep it in the band room, but we all had to get it out and put it away every evening for our rehearsals. We didn't actually practise very much whilst we were in Singapore because of all the parties that the officers were having, which Jeff had to attend, and which I had to work at. I was a little jealous as the other group had got themselves an old car. They had painted it with their name all over it and a union jack on the roof. They had also got some bookings, and a lot of people told me how good they had become.

I was still able to resume my scouting as there was a Scout group and Cub pack in the Aggie Weston's club which was in the middle of the married quarters. I became Shere Khan for the Cub pack. There was just one meeting a week and we never met at weekends because the children and parents often went away at weekends. It was a nice friendly group though, and I became quite friendly with some of the parents.

Because the Cubs were only one short evening per week I was still able to do my naval duties every day, my Blue Jacket band one day a week, and the group rehearsed every other evening. I was also serving in the Wardroom two to three evenings a week. The rest of the time I went out and socialised with my mess mates. Singapore was certainly like nothing I had ever known before.

The first night I went ashore with my mate Paddy O'Donell. Outside of the gate at Sembawang Village nearly every building was a bar. Paddy and myself decided we would try and make every bar our target. We started drinking at the first bar on the left and ordered a pint of Tiger beer each, which was served by a quite unfriendly, Oriental lady. We quickly decided that we would move next door to another bar.

The second bar was a little livelier than the first, and we met up with some more of our mates in this one. We also ended up having more beers than we intended. Eventually we left this bar to make our way to the next. Suddenly

71

Paddy started to follow a lady who, from behind, looked lovely, dressed very nicely and was wiggling her rear end sexily. Paddy said, "Bugger this drinking skylark, I'm going to have her tonight." He ran after her and shouted, "Oi, darling", in his thick Irish voice. She turned round and waited for Paddy and myself to reach her. She looked gorgeous. Paddy then asked her how much she would be for the night.

When she opened her mouth, you could hear that she wasn't all she seemed to be, and replied, "I'm a man, not a woman, and I will be ten dollars short time but fifty dollars all night, and I will give you a better time than any woman". Obviously Paddy and I thought this was very amusing, but we made our apologies and made for the next bar.

Paddy kept talking about her all the rest of the evening. We met up with some of our mates again and I told them what had happened. One of the older men, a leading steward called Tom, said that the man we had spoken to was a Kaiti, or ladyboy. He told us we would meet a lot more of them in Singapore. Tom had been to Singapore twice already so we knew he was right.

We all decided that we would go into Singapore itself. We piled into a couple of Taxis; they were black and yellow cabs and were all Mercedes. The drivers were mostly Indian gentlemen, with nothing on their feet.

"You want to go to the club in Singers", said the driver.

We all agreed that would be the best place to go. The driver of our car and the other one decided they would race each other, and they were lunatics. It didn't take us long to get to the Britannia club and it looked very nice. The fare was only about $3, which was less than 5 shillings. When we got inside there was a lovely bar, which was packed, so we all got a jug of Tiger beer each and went outside for a table. There was a football pitch outside with a sign stating that there would be a football match between HMS Bulwark and the RAF stationed in Singapore in two days time. We all agreed that, because we were not on duty then, we would go and watch.

After we'd had a few drinks we decided that we would make our way back to Sembawang. All along the street there were stalls selling food. Paddy and the others decided that they would have a curry at the stall that offered the cheapest. The ingredients were all mixed in a massive wok. I was not a curry man at all, so I looked around at other stalls and saw that one of them was making Chinese food. I noticed that he had trays of eggs and small baguettes. I asked the stall holder if he did the eggs in baguettes, and he said, "Yes, that will be $1." After he had finished doing the Chinese for someone he simply put two eggs in the same wok, cut open the baguette, and put the eggs inside. Well I can tell you it was the best I had ever had, and they called them egg banjos. I certainly had my share of them on our visits to Singapore.

As we walked through the dockyard we heard singing coming from near our ship and decided to head that way. We came across a building with hundreds of tables and chairs outside. It was full of matelots, mostly from the Bulwark but also from other ships. People were coming out of the building with jugs of beer and glasses. We all decided to get two jugs each and to join in with the singing. I can tell you all that there were songs being sung that I had never heard of, in fact some I haven't heard again. It was a brilliant night of entertainment, especially for us younger people. The night finished when the Naval Patrol came into the yard and told us all to leave but, believe me, I will never forget that night as long as I live.

The next morning my watch of stewards were on breakfast duties from 0800, where we had to serve any officers who were either on watch until 0800 or had simply laid in bed. Once they had been served it was our job to clear up the breakfast dishes and then go to our morning duties. I arrived in the Commanders' and Captain's flat (passage) to be met by the Dental Commander, who actually looked like a Gestapo Officer.

"Morning, young Mr Screech, I have some very important things for you to do for me today", he said. "In my cabin are my riding boots, which I expect to be gleaming. Also you will find my jodhpurs which are filthy and full of mud, which will have to be cleaned, along with my polo shirt which will need washing and ironing, and please don't forget my underwear and socks".

I had two other Commanders' cabins to clean as well, so I went to the Engineer Commander's cabin first. He had a very sparse cabin but had left one pair of shoes to clean, while his laundry was all bundled up for the Chinese laundry. I had to make his bunk up and then make the bunk into a sofa. This was all quite easy, though. The next cabin was Commander (L), the Electrical Commander. His cabin was very neat and he had left two pairs of shoes to be cleaned with his laundry which was to be made up, itemised and taken to the laundry. Again I had to make his bunk up and put it back to a sofa.

At ten that morning we all went to our mess for a cup of tea or coffee. We only had a quarter of an hour to get to our mess at the front of the ship to make our drink, drink it, then back to the officers' mess, which they called the bun run. I went straight to the Dental Commander's cabin since I only had three quarters of an hour to do his jobs. I was in the duty watch of stewards and had to have my own lunch, then clean up ready to serve the officers theirs. After the Pigs (officers) had eaten we had a quarter of an hour to change clothes and get back to report to the Duty Petty Officer Steward, who would allocate us work for the afternoon.

I was sent for by one of the Chief Stewards as soon as I got back. He shut the office door and told me to sit down and listen to him without saying a word. "What have you been doing all morning, young Screech? You only have three cabins to do and Commander D says you haven't touched his today."

I told the Chief about the amount of cleaning and washing he had given me to do and explained I was not able to do that much in the little time I had. The Chief told me that I could have the next two hours to get Commander D's cabin sorted. I tried my best, I really did, but I couldn't get the jodhpurs clean and could not get the stains off of the polo shirt. I cleaned the boots really quite well, I thought. His underwear was washed and left hanging by the scuttle (window) in his room to dry.

That evening, at about 1800, I'd just had my evening meal after serving the officers their tea. Over the tannoy came "Assistant Steward Screech, Commander D's cabin at the rush." I ran through 4-deck as quickly as I could and reached Commander D's cabin.

He was waiting for me and said, "My boots are still filthy, my jodhpurs are covered in mud and my polo shirt is not much better, Screech. As far as I am concerned I will be telling the Chief Steward to find me someone who is capable of doing this job, as you are obviously not."

I apologised to him but added that I thought he expected me to do too much, calling him Sir, and that I would be quite relieved to be taken off that job. He looked quite shocked by my reply, but I was happy that I said it.

I did do the officers' dinner that night, but asked the duty P.O. if I could possibly do the wash-up with my mate Johnny. He was always good for laugh, he was from Newcastle and nothing or nobody bothered Johnny. We were having a laugh when Johnny said, "Here take one of these purple hearts, it will make you feel much better, and tonight will go faster."

All of Johnny's mates used to take these but it was something that I'd never wanted to try, so I pretended to take it but threw it away. Then I had to pretend I was as high as Johnny and his mates. I don't think I was being a prude but my Dad was an ex-Master-at-Arms and a serving policeman and he always warned me against taking drugs.

The next day we had the early breakfasts and the morning shakes to do. We had to carry a four pint tea pot, with a brass bowl (finger bowl) in place of a lid to carry the sugar in with an EPNS tea spoon to pour out sugar and stir. I had 845 pilots to shake. Most of them were alright actually, in fact they were nearly all quite funny.

When the officers shakes were done, we all tried to grab a cup of tea before serving breakfast to them. At 0745 the next lot of flunkies relieved us so that we could have our breakfasts. Then the pattern would start all over again, work on the officers' cabins, or in the officers' mess, or in the bar, or up in the ACRB (Aircrew Refreshment Bar). I was back to the Commanders' cabins. Luckily, the Dental Commander had not been playing polo so there were no polo boots, jodhpurs, or polo shirt to clean. Instead, the miserable person had left out two more pairs of shoes and a pair of sandals to clean along with, of course, his underwear. Once again it took too long to do his cabin so I went to the Chief Steward and told him that I would like to be considered for another job on the ship, anywhere away from the Commander Dentist.

Whilst I was in the office one of the Petty Officer Stewards, Bob Sands, said, "Actually, Chief, there has been a signal out for some time about changes in how officers are to be looked after. It's a DCI (Defence Council Instruction) and says that changes have come about, and that officers can't get the personal treatment from now on unless they are prepared to pay for those services."

The Chief gave P.O. Sands a dirty look and said, "Okay, we will look into it." He then told me that I was to stick with doing it in the meantime, and he would give me extra time in the afternoons when I was duty or standby to just do his stuff.

Tim Jewell was the singer of Four Jacks and a Knave, he also played the trumpet, and I had moaned to Tim a few times about how this dental bloke was treating me. Tim was a writer in his day job, working in the Captain's office.

That night at our rehearsal he said to me, "You know that business you told me about with the Dentist? Well, there has been a DCI out for some time that officers are now not entitled to personal valeting and such services. But if they were to pay individually for these services to the steward, then that would be permitted." Tim also told me that the DCI came out before we left the UK.

As you can imagine, I was straight to the Chief's office the next morning. He was flapping about and saying to me, "Yes, but that hasn't come in yet."

I told him that he was wrong and that anyone beneath the Captain was not entitled. I was so happy when I then went to the cabins and saw that there were boots, jodhpurs and the like left out for me to do and I could ignore them. I carried out the rest of my duties, went for my lunch, got changed into my white shorts and white front (turned to) and started work in the officers' dining room. I had only been in the Wardroom for ten minutes when the chief steward came into the dining room, pointed at me and called me out. I followed and he led me to the Commander Dentist's cabin.

The Commander was in the cabin and he told the Chief and me to go inside. He directed his question at me, saying, "What have I ever done to you, Screech, that you feel you can sacrifice your career in the Navy by refusing to do your work?"

I plucked up the courage to answer him and said, "There is a DCI out, Sir, that says I don't have to do this kind of work unless I get paid by the officer concerned."

He then turned round to the Chief and asked if that was true. The Chief replied that it was true, and that he had just found out.

"Okay", said the Commander, "In that case I will pay you for doing it."

There was no agreement about how much he would pay me, or how often. The Chief told me to get back to work and said he would discuss it with me later. That day, when I went back to work in the afternoon, I was told to do the work for the dentist. I did it and kept thinking, well, I am going to get paid for this. I will tell you later how I got on with this.

After spending a couple of weeks in Singapore, which was a fantastic time, we were then sailing for Hong Kong. We were going to take a two week stay in Hong Kong, then go back to Singapore to pick up 42 Commando and take them to Brisbane, Australia with us. So we took the Commandos with us to Labuan to start with, then we were taking them back to Singapore so they could prepare for Australia, and because most of them were married and their wives were with them, they could say their goodbyes.

Labuan was a part of Borneo as far as I was aware. We were carrying out some exercises on the way, taking the Marines to different places, then bringing them back. Being a non-combatant, we had to do the first aid and stretcher parties from the flight deck to the sick bay. It was heavy and dirty work. They had made up the Marines as if they were injured, and we had to treat them as such until we off-loaded them at the sick bay. The first case I had was a Marine who was supposed to have his stomach hanging out. We were told to push his stomach back in and cover the injury with crepe bandages and field dressings. Then we had to take him down gently via the aircraft lift to the sick bay. We were told we had done a good job, but to be honest it made me feel quite sick.

After the exercises we were to call into Labuan and there was no official leave allowed. However, the ships football team were going to have a football match against a local team and the Blue Jacket band were going to play at half time. This was quite exciting as we were going ashore, even if for a short time, and we knew the rest of the ship's company were not going ashore.

The day went well and we even beat the locals 10-1. At half time we played some music and that was it. However, at the end of the game the ship's Commander, who was with us, said that we could have a run ashore as long as someone could bring our musical instruments back to the ship. I was the only bandsman who stayed, but there was an electrician football player and a Marine football player who also said they would like to stay. We also had an American sailor onboard who was on loan to the ship and decided to stay as well. The four of us went into town where there were no bars to speak of, and just roadside stalls which sold Tiger beer, so we stayed at one of those stalls and drank beer.

After a while a man came to us and said, "You would like to go to a dance? I will organise for you." We all agreed, and before we knew where we were a taxi had come for us. It was dirt cheap and not too far. When we arrived at the dance, it was strange to see, but there were only women and young girls there. We went in and they were selling Tiger beer very cheaply, so we just sat drinking and, after a couple of hours, decided to leave.

There were no taxis outside the dancehall, although there was an open backed lorry. The American sailor got into the driver's seat and started the vehicle. The Marine got in beside him and they started to pull away. The electrician and I jumped on the back of the lorry and we moved off down the road. On the way into the town there were a number of roundabouts, the American was obviously not used to them and just went across the top of them, throwing us two in the back all over the place. We were then being followed by two police cars with the sirens going. The driver started to go faster and faster. The two of us in the back were then thrown out of the lorry, but the police went straight past us and kept chasing the lorry.

We made our way to the pickup point to take the bus back to the ship. Someone was counting us on to make sure we were all ready to go back. The two guys from the lorry were not back though, and I haven't seen or heard of them since.

I have seen the electrician on a couple of occasions since, in fact I saw him a few years later whilst on another ship in Gibraltar, but never found out his name.

We dropped off the Marines at Singapore and had another week alongside, enjoying our time. I personally had been practising sailing in boson dinghies and entered into the 'Round Singapore Island' race. My crew was a young boy whose father was a dentist on another ship. He was probably more experienced than I was at sailing. We won the race in our class of boat which was quite an achievement. Apart from the sailing, most of my spare time was taken up doing the naval band, Four Jacks and a Knave, and of course going to help out with the cub pack.

Before long we were ready to leave Singapore with the Commandos on board. The ship seemed so crowded once they were on board, with all their kit, lorries and Land Rovers taking up all the spare space. It was all very uncomfortable. When there was no flying, the flight deck was packed with Marines sunbathing and taking up all the extra spaces. Meals became difficult because the Marines were first in the queue, even with us having different timed meals so we could go and serve the officers, you could guarantee the front of the queues would be full of Marines. It mostly meant that we didn't have time to finish ours. To make matters worse, the Marine officers were the first into the dining room and they had no Marines to serve them, the only thing they put into it was giving us a Marine each mealtime to help with the washing up. To be honest these Marines didn't give monkeys and were not very helpful.

Still, we were on our way to Brisbane so we could put up with the hardships to an extent. We also had hands to bathe events on the way. The ship came to a stop, the ship's boats were lowered, then they made an announcement over the ships tannoy. "Hands to bathe, hands to bathe", after which people were jumping over the side of the ship from the decks on four deck.

My mate Paddy said, "Bugger that, let's just jump in from here on the flight deck."

This we did and, although we heard people shouting for us to stop, we still carried on, after which other people started to follow us. I can tell you I would never do that again, I went so far under the sea that I didn't think I would ever get back again, and my feet really stang. Once I surfaced, one of the sea boats was waiting for me. I was told to get in the boat and they picked up one or two others before taking us back to the side of ship. We had to climb up the rope ladder and were then escorted, still soaking wet, to the Regulating Office.

Once there we were lined up outside and a Regulating Petty Officer came out to us, took all our names and ranks, and told us we were in trouble for jumping off the flight deck. We had to go and change into our work clothes and reported back to the Regulating Office in an hour. I was the only one from my mess that was caught, and I was the laughing stock.

We all had to go to the Officer of the Day's table for him to decide if we should go any further up the line of the Commander's table, then possibly the Captain's table. We all got three days number nines (extra work and stoppage of leave). Leading Hands that were guilty were given five days stoppage of leave. Everyone that was entitled to rum was also given three days stoppage of grog. I was too young anyway. The punishment flew past as I was given my extra work in the officer's mess so it was easy, and we were at sea so we could not go ashore anyway.

At that time Mao Tse Tung was playing up in China and had made all sorts of threats to Britain. The Chinese in Hong Kong were doing the occasional rioting, so we were all put into squads with Marines and had to practise marching into Hong Kong and break up rioters. We non-combatants were in the centre of these platoons, carrying stretchers. It was quite exciting, though when we got to Hong Kong I think it had all died down. Mao Tse Tung said that he was not scared of the Bulwark as it was just a paper tiger.

We enjoyed our visit to Hong Kong and got a booking at the Top Hat nightclub to play with Four Jacks and a Knave. We took over from a Chinese band who, to be honest, could not hold a tune, so we went down really well. The Missing Lynx were also playing in another nightclub, and both bands were going down really well. Other nightclub owners used to come and watch us and were forever making us offers to play at their clubs. We had a really good offer from the Cave nightclub. We agreed, through Jeff, to accept it.

The night we started, there were outside advertisements about us with photos and the times we were playing. The place was crowded when we arrived and some of our bosses were there, including my Divisional Officer LT (Ducky) Warren who was there with P.O. STD Bob Sands. We had a really good night and played a number of Beatles and Monkees songs.

We didn't know that some producers from Hong Kong television were there. They had a few words with Jeff during our break and he came back onstage after the break with a great big smile on his face. He didn't say anything at the time, but he whispered to each of us that we were in for a surprise at the end of the night. After we finished playing we sat around the table having a beer. Jeff told us then that the TV station wanted us to play on their version of Ready Steady Go two days later, and we would be appearing live. Wow, we were all over the moon and very excited! Jeff told us that he would speak to the Captain about us having time off work to rehearse for the next couple of days. He said he had already spoken to Lt Warren, and he'd agreed to let me have the time off.

The next day the Captain made an announcement over the ships system to tell everyone what we were doing. We spent all day rehearsing and, in the evening, we had to go back to the club for an agreed performance. The club actually doubled our wages from then on so it was all good. That night we had to pack up my drum kit and all the other equipment and get it back to the ship.

The next day we once again rehearsed what we would be playing on the television. At 1600 that day we packed all our stuff into the ship's Land Rover and were off to the studio. When we got there the studio staff showed us where to set up our gear. I've got to say that, at this stage, the studio staff were not very friendly nor very helpful. We started playing and didn't even realise we were already live on the telly. When we finished our session we were rushed out whilst another band started to set up in the same place as we had just been playing. We were then rushed out of the studios and took our kit back to the nightclub and set it all up again ready for another performance.

At the end of the night Jeff told us that we were going for a meal on a sampan. This was so interesting and, as we went around the harbour, different little sampans came alongside us. They were offering us food that was often caught live, then cooked and served to us on our boat. Most of the band chose what lobster they wanted but, of course, I just had vegetables and a bit of chicken. It was a great night and we got back to the ship at about 0400. We were given the next day off, so mostly slept until we went back to the Cave for our last performance before sailing for Brisbane. That night we played as usual and, during the interval, Jeff introduced us to an Australian lady who had heard about us and wanted us to appear on television in Brisbane.

Before arriving in Brisbane we had to have the usual exercises with the Australian Navy. This naturally meant going back to normal duties and I was also back with doing the Commanders' cabins and, of course, the dentist's washing and cleaning. It seemed that no one had been doing it for him whilst I had been doing other things, so much so that there were piles of washing and shoe cleaning, plus his polo boots were filthy. I washed his gear and hung it all over his cabin, I knew he wouldn't be happy with this but I didn't care less.

I made sure that, when I was on duty, I was able to spend time out in the afternoons. We also had to rehearse playing with the band and the Royal Marine volunteer pipe band, ready to do a march through the centre of Brisbane. It was very hard at first as we were a brass band and some of the music was for pipe bands, also their drummers played on different sounding drums with very much more prominent snares. Don't get me wrong though, those drummers were excellent.

On our arrival in Brisbane we had to play on the flight deck and the Marines were also playing there, although we did not play together. As we were going alongside there were hundreds of people waiting for us, particularly women, who were all screaming and shouting to us. Hundreds of people seemed to be coming aboard as soon as we got in.

Most of the ship's company and Royal Marines were getting ready to go ashore as soon as they could but, as ever, we stewards had to prepare for the officers' cocktail party, which we called their Cock and Arse party. We had to set up bars on the flight deck and get all the booze up with the glasses and jugs, lemons cut, silver salvers cleaned etc.

That evening the Cock and Arse was going very well, nearly all the officers that were straight had met young ladies and, as soon as they could, were going ashore with them. We had to keep serving hot and cold snacks with their drinks. Some of the stewards had bottles of booze stuck inside their stockings, which they were taking to the stewards mess ready for the cooks and stewards party afterwards. In fact, after the officers' party, whilst the younger stewards were clearing everything up, most of the older stewards had disappeared down the mess and had started their parties.

We had finished the clear up at about 2200 and it was too late for any of us to go ashore. To be honest, by the time we had finished, we were too shattered anyway and, when we got to the mess, most of the older guys were well stoned and didn't want to give any of us a drink. The Regulating Branch was quite busy arresting drunks coming back to the ship and also the drunks in our mess. Not a lot of sleep took place in our mess that night.

The next morning we were practising for the march through Brisbane with the pipe band. It was even sounding quite good. We were playing a bit, then the Marines played their bit, and it all seemed to fit in very well. After lunch we had to get into our best uniforms and the Marines got into their kilts. We then loaded all of the instruments onto an Australian Army lorry, got ourselves onto a couple of Army coaches, and headed for the city centre.

When we arrived there we got our instruments together. We then formed up, with us at the front and the Marines at the rear. Crowds were forming at the start and, once we started playing, the crowds cheered. It was a wonderful feeling, I can tell you. We marched through the city as crowds were building up, all standing and cheering, and I had never experienced anything like it before.

When we had finished the Navy band loaded our instruments back on the lorry. The Marine pipe band played some more tunes as the crowd gathered round them, they were brilliant, and none of them were really recognised musicians since they were Royal Marine Commandos. This was just a part time thing for them, the same as us, though they were far better. Mind you, they were stationed in Singapore with their families and did not have a lot to do there but play music. We all headed back to the ship in the coach and unloaded our instruments. We were then free to go back into the city.

I went ashore with the group to see if we could find a gig to play at. The television appearance seemed to come to nothing, even though we had a good write up in the local papers. Instead, we ended up going for a nice steak meal. I had a T-bone steak and it was the best I'd ever had. In the restaurant there were some families eating and I noticed that two boys at one table were dressed in cub scout uniforms. I got chatting to their parents and they told me that the cub pack met in a small hall near where the ship was berthed, and they had a meeting on the Monday night. That evening we had a Deep Sea Scout meeting on the ship and decided that we would pay a visit on the Monday.

Six of us donned our scout uniforms on the Monday evening and off we went. We took a lot of stick from other members of the ship's company because of our uniforms, but we were pretty well used to that. We went to the scout hut and it was halfway through the cub meeting, so we organised a couple of games for them which were well appreciated. We were then asked if we would stay for the scout meeting and organise some games for them, which of course we did. It was a really good night and there must have been around sixty scouts there.

At the end of the evening we were all invited to one of the leader's homes for a barbeque. We had a fabulous evening with loads of food and gallons of beer; it was another really good night.

We were in Brisbane for a few more days and spent most of our time with the Australian leaders. On the last night, when we had arrived back on the ship, there was a scruffy man standing on the Jetty who asked if we could take him on the ship as he was a sailor who had deserted when his ship was there. We took him up the gangway and one of our lot went to see the Officer of the Watch to tell him what the scruff had told us. The Reggies were called and he was escorted to the Master at Arms office. He was then put in cells. He was coming back to Singapore with us, where he would have to get his punishment at the Naval base. We heard later that he was sentenced to 42 days at Stone Cutters Island in Hong Kong, which was a service detention centre. From there he was discharged and flown back to the UK.

The next morning another problem occurred as the majority of the 40 Commando pipe band had not returned from shore. It turned out that the majority of them had found young ladies and decided they were not coming back. The ship did not sail on time as the Captain decided he would give them a little longer, and most of them had wives and families back in Singapore so it was going to be a bit of an embarrassment to the Captain, the ship, and the British government. We eventually sailed, yet most of the Marines had not made it. Although it was mentioned over the ship's tannoy, not too much was made of it.

We went straight to Singapore and several meetings took place in different places on the ship to discuss what had happened, though it was kept very private and we were not given any more information. We did see the Marines leave the ship, and they were also taking the missing Marines' kit with them. The pipe band was obviously disbanded and I heard that they all went home more or less straight away.

Whilst in Singapore I, like most of the sailors, went to Neesoon Village where some of the sailors took to going to Virgin's Corner, a place where the older and cheaper prostitutes did their business. I had to go to Shaky Joe's tattoo shop to have a tattoo of a Kangaroo put onto my right arm. I wanted to go back to Johnny Gurkha's to have it really but he was too busy. So I went to Shaky Joe's and had the Kangaroo tattooed on my right arm. He really made a mess of it, but at the time I was too drunk to notice. It wasn't until the next morning it was pointed out to me that the Australian flag was wrong, and the baby Kangaroo was in the wrong place and the Mother Kangaroo's arms were too long.

After two weeks I had to go back to Johnny Gurkha's and asked him if he could do anything to help me. He said there was little he could do but he would try his best. He did the best he could but it was never brilliant.

We then went back to sea for more exercises before heading back to Hong Kong for Christmas. It was also going to be my twentieth birthday, which meant my first tot. Life at sea in this period was pretty mundane. My biggest problem was the guy who worked in the bridge mess. He used to follow me around and try to persuade me to go and see him at the bridge mess since he spent all his spare time there as well as his working time.

One of the other young stewards told me to be careful as he'd had to go to the bridge mess to take some food there and Scammell would try to get him to do strange things with him. I got so fed up with it all that I told a couple of the Senior Leading Hands in the mess, who just advised me to keep away from him. I then went to see the Catholic Priest about him. He was very nice and told me that he would have words with our Divisional Officer and the Church of England vicar. He said not to worry as it would all be sorted out. Unfortunately it wasn't, he started to quite openly pick on me, and kept touching my bum.

One day one of the P.O. stewards told me I had to go to the bridge mess with some cucumber so the steward there could make some sandwiches for afternoon tea. I told him I didn't want to go, so he asked me why. I told him what he had been doing to me and some other stewards.

He said, "Don't be stupid, Screech, get up there with the cucumber."

I did as I was told and went up to the bridge mess. I thought Scammel would be in the mess itself, writing or doing something else. I tried the door handle but the door was locked. I opened the pantry door instead, he wasn't there either, but I heard a noise coming from inside the mess. I then opened the hatch that went inside. To my horror, Scammel had a knife pointing at one of my mate's neck. He had him lying on the sofa while he was crouched over and was telling him to get his clothes off. I then shouted at Scammel to get off my mate. I tried to push myself through the hatch and, though I was tiny, I struggled and Scammel ran towards me with the knife.

My mate then jumped on his back and pulled him by his neck to the ground just as I got through the hatch. I got hold of the knife and threw it through the open hatch. My mate, Mick, then unlocked the mess door and ran out into the passageway, calling for help. A couple of lads came rushing to the mess and bolted in.

Scammel was acting as if everything was normal, and said, "Cor! That was a laugh, wasn't it?"

Mick and I went down to the Wardroom and told the P.O. steward what had happened. He said to go and have a cup of tea so he could talk to Scammel. I wasn't happy with that and said to Mick that I was going to the Regulating Office to report it to the Joss (Master-At-Arms). Mick wouldn't come with me.

"I don't want to get anyone in the shit", he said.

So I went on my own. I told the duty Regulating P.O. what had happened. He went to the bridge mess and brought Scammel down. I was sent away and thought that would be the end of it. Mick was called to the Regulating Office and questioned. Then he came back to the Wardroom and said he'd told them nothing had happened.

That evening I was called to the Regulating Office where they told me off for telling lies and trying to get someone in trouble. I couldn't believe he was getting away with it. I went back to the Wardroom to serve dinner. During dinner, Scammel came into the mess, pitched up to me and whispered in my ear, "You can't get me, Screech, I've got too many friends on here. You be careful because I will get you, one way or another, you just wait. Be careful when you go to your bunk at night."

For the rest of the time on our travel to Hong Kong, I tried to keep out of his way as much as I could. Every time I came across him I tried to avoid eye contact but he would make a point of bumping into me, and saying things like, "Sorry, Darling", or "Whoops, silly me." He was really making my life a misery but no one would listen to me. The night before we got into Hong Kong, the mess was all asleep when, at about two in the morning, I was woken by Scammel bending over my bunk and grabbing hold of my private parts. I jumped up and shouted at him to get off me and leave me alone. He casually stood up and said to the rest of the mess, "It's okay, lads, it's just Screech being stupid again."

Luckily there was a leading steward in the bunk opposite mine, he got up and said, "I saw everything you did, Scammel, so I am going to troop you first thing in the morning." The next morning Scammel was taken to the Regulating Office. He was then put in the cells until we got into Hong Kong. As soon as we arrived alongside, Scammel was taken ashore by the Naval patrol who took him away to HMS Tamar.

Some of the people in the mess apologised to me, and when I went to the Wardroom, the C.P.O. apologised for not believing me. Most of the lads were pleased and it was like having a weight off their shoulders. The Chief told me to take a couple of days off, so I went to see my Aunt Nancy and her husband, George. I went the next day too, and then I was due to work over Christmas. Some of the lads took the opportunity to have a couple of days in the China Fleet Club. On Boxing Day I went back to Nancy and George's and had a lovely time. It was going through my mind what was going to happen to Scammel, though. Nancy told me that I had to go over to their place on my birthday as we would have a lovely party. I promised I would be there at 1930 on the second.

The next day was the day I was to receive my first tot. I didn't know the format of what happened, I was just told that I had to be in the mess at 1200 sharp. At 1200 I was sat in the senior of the stewards part of the mess. They told me to sit down next to the senior killick and a big mug was placed in front of me. I asked what that was about, but was told to wait and see. Just after 1200 one of the killicks and an older steward called Mick Champ bought a great big fanny in the mess and put it on the table.

The killick picked up a board with all our names on. Mick picked up the mug that I had, he put rum into the brass issue mug and then poured it into my mug. I had to offer Mick and the ticker off a sip, which I did. Then everyone else was lining up for their tot. They gave the ticker off a sip, then Mick, and then they put a lot of grog in my mug and wished me a happy birthday. This mug was filled twice and I was expected to drink it all.

By the time I had started on the second mugful I asked Billy McCabe if he would make sure that, if I went to sleep, I was up for 1800 as I had to go to see my Aunt. I did remember going to bed, and I remember Billy waking me up, saying "Come on, Mick, it's 1800.

I jumped out of bed and said, "Shit, I've got to get to Kowloon by 1930."

Bill said, "I wouldn't rush...that was yesterday."

I had slept right through my birthday afternoon, right through the night and all the next day. I got showered and dressed and made for Kowloon to apologise to Nancy and George. Nancy was very upset, but George, being an ex-matelot, understood. When I went back to the ship that night that was the last time I'd see Nancy and George for five years.

We took some Gurkhas and other soldiers on board the next morning. They were going to do an exercise in Ghan. They were alright, we even had some Gurkhas working in the officer's mess and, although they weren't trained stewards, they were good at what they did. They also put three pongoes (soldiers) in the pot wash, so for a couple of days we had an easy time. At tot time the Gurkhas were given their tots on the quarterdeck. They didn't drink and invited some of the crew to have some grog with them. A lot of us went up there and had a large amount of rum. The patrolmen quickly got wind of it, they all came up to the quarterdeck and told us to go away. What rum was left was thrown over the side.

After the exercise we went back to Singapore, dropped off our guests and were to spend a certain amount of ships maintenance. Some of us stewards were told we had better get our best suits ready as there was going to be a court martial in the barracks in a couple of days. Apparently Scammel had been flown back to Singapore to be court martialled. On the day of his court martial there were quite a number of people attending, including fleet air arm guys, seamen, stokers officers and one Chinese laundryman all waiting to give evidence against him.

When they had decided he was guilty, no one told us what he'd got. We all returned to the ship and there was lots of talk about what he had done to everyone. Two days after it was over my Divisional Officer sent for me and told me that he had been given 60 days in detention in Portsmouth and dishonourably discharged from the Navy. When he spoke at the end he told people there that some of us would suffer when he had gone, especially Screech. The ship was due to pick up a lot of servicemen from Aden on the way home as Britain was pulling out. I told Lt. Warren that it left me in fear, and would there be any chance that I could fly home. He said he doubted it, but he would check.

The next day I was sent to see the Captain. He asked if I felt safe and I replied that, in all honesty, I didn't as there were still friends of Scammels on board, including officers and senior rates. A day later I had to say goodbye to everyone as I was moving to the barracks until I flew home. I went to say goodbye to the Commanders I'd looked after, including the dentist as he still owed me some money. He was in his cabin so I knocked on his door and he signalled for me to go in, pointing to his jodhpurs and saying, "These need doing, Screech."

I replied, "Sorry, Sir, but I'm afraid I am leaving the ship, and you owe me some money, Sir."

"Ah, yes! Yes, Screech." He opened his drawer and said, "There you are, young man, a three penny piece for you."

"Thank you, Sir", I said before I dropped the money on the floor and walked away.

I told the Chief what happened and he said, "Well, from now on he won't have any of the staff to do it for him."

I managed to sell the two drum kits I had and packed my bags ready for my move. The next day I watched from the jetty as the ship sailed away. All I was thinking was 'I hate the bloody Navy, my second sea going ship, which I had been bullied on'. What a life!

Chapter Four

Threats, Marriage, Promotion, HMS Osprey

After having some leave I then had a letter from the Ministry of Defence to say I was to join HMS Osprey, Portland Naval Air Station, on the 26th July 1967. That was fairly good for me as my fiancée, Edwina, lived in Taunton, some 50 miles away. However, on Monday 24th July, I had to report to the M.O.D. in Whitehall to see a Mr Green. I was both anxious and worried about this, but I put on a collar and tie and did as I was asked.

At exactly 1000 Mr Green appeared and led me to an office. I sat down and he could see my anxiety. He said, "Don't worry, Steward Screech, I just have to check on how you're feeling and to make sure you are still going to be able to serve your country without giving any information to anyone."

I informed him that I was very confident that I could carry on serving and that I wouldn't give anyone any information that I may receive. He seemed to accept what I had said and then he warned me that a certain person had told everyone that I and a few other people had been threatened by Mr Scammel, and that if he made contact with me I was to inform the police or the Naval authorities immediately. I assured him that I would. I left there thinking that I didn't know what I should do, should I leave the Navy or continue?

I went home and told my parents what had been said. My dad, who was a police sergeant, thought about it for a while and said, "Stick with it, son, but do as he told you and, if you get approached, do as he said."

My mum went into panic mode and said, "If I were you I would leave the Navy and come home."

I decided that I would do as my dad said and go back to face whatever came up.

So there it was, I joined HMS Osprey and was shown to my accommodation. It was in a row of mess decks on the side of a hill and we officer stewards were in the deck at the top two messes. I was allocated a bed which was a bunk but all single in a row. I had a locker next to it and it all seemed quite nice. I then had to go down to the air station to the Regulating Office where they set me on my joining routine, which entailed going to the pay office, the stores office for bedding etc. before I had to go to the sick bay, the dentists and other offices.

Finally I had to report to the chief steward who introduced me to my divisional officer. He was obviously aware of my visit to Whitehall, the threats that had been made and mostly about my commission on the Bulwark. He seemed a very nice officer. The chief told me to go back to the Regulating Office with my joining routine completed, then to get to know my mess mates, get my kit put away and relax. This I did and I got to know some of the guys quite well. I didn't mention my experiences on the Bulwark since I thought people were bound to bring it all up at some stage. That night, after ringing my fiancée, a few of us went to the bar.

My life at Osprey was going fairly well and, whenever I could, I would go to see my fiancée in Taunton. We were planning our marriage for January 1968. I had put my name down for a married quarter and was advised that I may have a long wait. I then decided that if I got a rented flat in Weymouth, the Navy would subsidise me for living out as there was a shortage of accommodation at Osprey. While I was looking out for a flat I lived a normal life of going ashore some nights. I decided that it was best to go on a bus that went from Osprey into Weymouth.

One afternoon one of the stewards, who had been ashore to the betting office, came up to me and asked if I knew a guy called Scammel. I told him I did and he said that he'd met a bloke in the betting office who said that he had served with me on my last ship. He'd also heard that I had joined Osprey and would love to go for a drink with me sometime. He said that if I was to go ashore the next day he would meet me outside the dockyard gate at 1900 the next day. I didn't know if this lad had found out about Scammel from somewhere or whether he was genuine. I decided to get on the bus and have a look outside the gate.

Sure enough, I sat upstairs on the bus and looked out of the window when we got to the gate. Standing there was

Scammel. I went back to the camp straight away and made my way to the Wardroom, askinp one of the Stewards if he could look for the boss for me. The boss came to see me at the back of the Wardroom. I explained to him what had happened. He then said he would report it to the Naval patrolmen. He suggested that I stay in Osprey for the rest of the evening.

The next day, several of the lads that had gone ashore came to me and said they met a bloke called Scammel who was asking after me. I went to the boss and asked if he had reported Scammel to the Naval patrol. He said he had but they couldn't find him, instead they were going to report the contact to the civilian police. I'm thankful to say I never heard from or about Scammel from that day onwards.

I was getting on well at Osprey, I was about to get promoted alongside two good friends. We were going to the Captain's table the following morning, so we decided we would go ashore but stay in Portland to make sure we behaved and got our hooks the next day. We had a better run ashore than we expected and all got fairly drunk. We decided we would walk back to Osprey to sober us up a bit.

Just before we got to the dockyard gate we came across Bernard's Naval Tailors shop. I had been having a row with Bernard's as they'd ripped me off a couple of years before. As we got to the shop doorway I said to the other two, "I'm going to have a pee through their letterbox."

We all went into the doorway. I decided not to pee in their letterbox but to do one against their door instead. This I proceeded to do. We were all laughing when suddenly a Naval patrol van pulled up beside us. Two patrolmen got out, they asked for our ID cards. They took them off us then asked if we knew where the nearest toilet was, which we all said we did. They then put us in the van and took us to Osprey. They kept our ID cards and we were told we had to report to the Regulating Office at 0800 the next morning where we would be on the Officer of the Day's defaulters.

When we got back to the mess we discussed our case for the next day. I said that I was going to plead not guilty, as they had no proof that we had done it. The other two said that, even though they didn't do it, they were going to plead guilty as they wouldn't get too much punishment. The next day we went to the Officer of the Day in our working clothes (no. eights). We went in together and they both pleaded guilty while I pleaded not guilty. We were all told we would have Commander's table. At about 0900 we had to have our best uniforms on and waited outside for Commander's defaulters.

This time we had to go in one at a time. Brum Teedwell was first and he came out having received seven days number nine punishment (extra work and stoppage of leave). After that, Roger Pavey went in and he got the same as Brum. Then it was my turn, I pleaded not guilty and told the Commander that I would defend myself. I was given the Captain's table at 1000. I was the first defaulter to be called in. I pleaded not guilty and also told the Captain that none of us were guilty as it was not possible. The leading patrolman had said in his statement that, although he hadn't seen us, there was urine running down the left hand side of the porch. I was then asked if I would like to question the leading patrolman. I said the only question I had was 'did you say the urine was running down the left hand side of the doorway', to which the patrolman said yes. I then said to the Captain, "I would like to show you, Sir, that, because it was on a slight incline, any urine would have run down the right hand side."

The Captain then spoke to his officers. He turned around to me and said, "Case dismissed, well done, Steward Screech." After all the other men had finished with the Captain, I was called in again and had to salute. The Captain said "Steward Screech, you are promoted to Acting Leading Steward as from this date." You can imagine how that went down with the other two, especially as they hadn't done anything at all.

I managed to get a flat in Abbotsbury Road in Weymouth. It wasn't bad but the box used to eat coins for the electric. We also had a television which was a 'feed me' machine. Edwina came down to see it and, although it wasn't brilliant, she didn't mind until we got a married quarter. We gradually got things ready for after we were married and would move in. There was a prostitute who lived upstairs and, every time she bought clients back, her bed used to pound up and down and, depending who her customer was, there was a lot of grunting and moaning. I hoped it wouldn't be long before we got a married quarter.

We were married on the 20th January 1968 and, on Monday 22nd, we were on the train back to Weymouth. We moved in to our little flat and it was freezing. We had been given an electric blanket as a wedding gift. I had to put a plug on it, which was the only do-it-yourself my dad had ever taught me. We put the blanket on the bed and I put the plug into the socket. The minute I had got the plug in, I was thrown right across the room. My first thought was did I put the plug on right, or it was a rogue blanket. When I had sorted myself out I looked at the wall and it was soaking wet.

Within two months I was informed that we had been given a married quarter in Portland. We had been given a brand new top floor flat in Odgers Court, Woolacombe Road East Cliff. We were very impressed with all the brand new bedding, crockery and cutlery, all brand new furniture, it was lovely. We introduced ourselves to our neighbours; he was a fleet air arm guy. They were a bit older than us but they were very nice. Because we didn't have things like washing machines, fridges, freezers etc. we had to make do. We had a nice balcony which looked over the cliff, and that was where we kept our milk in a bucket and where we kept most of our dairy products.

Edwina, my wife, had got a job when we were in Weymouth at one of Debenhams stores called Bennets.

She didn't like it much. In Taunton she worked in Debenhams offices, so this was very different. She also had to get a bus both ways and going down the big hill from the top to the bottom used to frighten her to death. Of course she had to work every other Saturday, which she'd never had to work in Taunton. Still, we settled in quite nicely. Family members came to stay with us, as did friends, and we sometimes caught a bus to Taunton.

I bought some motorcycles and a Ford Popular car with the intention of doing it up, but every time we went out it was by bus. We had made friends with a leading chef who I worked with. They had a married quarter on the patch and they would sometimes take us out in their three wheeler car. I loved it but Edwina was more scared going down the hill in that car than on the bus.

Once the summer was over I got a draft to HMS Eagle. I had to join it in Plymouth in January 1969. There was going to be a club in Easton which was going to be just for future Eagle crew. It was a hall that had been abandoned for a fair while by the Army cadets. We had a meeting one day to sort out the positions in the club, such as chairman, treasurer, social secretary etc. I was elected as the chairman, which surprised me with all the fleet air arm guys that were joining.

We cleared the rooms of rubbish, decorated it and did up the outside to enable people to get in. It wasn't long before we got the NAAFI involved to run the bar for us and the social sec. organised some very good, established entertainers. We were up and running with 300+ members and were filling the club every night. We allowed civilian women to join after paying a £2 joining fee. I loved it, but couldn't afford to go every night.

When we went on Christmas leave we moved in with my mother-in-law back in Taunton. My father-in-law had passed away in the April, so she had a spare room as Edwina's sister had gone to college in Gloucester. They were building some new houses near my mother-in-law's so we had a look with a view to buying one. Good old mother-in-law lent us the deposit we needed and we arranged a mortgage. The house would be built before Christmas. My new adventure was about to begin.

Chapter Five

United States and HMS Eagle

Like joining the Bulwark, a lot of the ship's company joined the same day. The squadrons joined later, mostly before their aeroplanes came on board. It was pandemonium as so many of us were wandering around the ship looking for our new mess decks. We were quite lucky because our mess was along the main deck to 'S' section, towards the back of the ship. As we entered the mess we were met by the leading hand of the mess, an old and bold two badge killick. He was quite a big but well-built man, who was well organised. When we gave our name, he would tell one of the young lads helping him to take us and show us our bunk and locker. The keys were already in the lockers so it was all pretty smooth.

Round the back of the mess was the officers cooks' section, which was slightly smaller. Around the top of that were some stewards and then, in the main part of the mess, were all stewards down to the last section which was the leading stewards section, which I was put in. It had a bigger recreation space than the rest of the mess, and I for one was quite happy to be in there. The lockers were all in a row along the forward side of the mess, and mine was luckily right near my bunk.

The only issue with my bunk was that there was a man in the top bunk above me. He only had about a foot of space

111

above him and would have to climb up the bottom bunk and mine to get into his. There was about two feet above my bunk. Below me was another bunk which was static and doubled up as a seating area during the day. This meant that every morning the bottom bunk would have to cover his bedding over in a plastic cover. My bunk also had to be put in a plastic cover and my bunk pulled over at daytime to become the back of the seat. The top bunk guy, despite being the person with the least room, only had to cover his bed.

Once we had settled down we had to go to the Wardroom to be given our jobs. We were introduced to the two Chief Stewards and the four Petty Officer Stewards. There were about a hundred stewards in all. Some were put as cabin stewards, some as bar stewards, some as pantry stewards and some were to report to the junior rates dining room to work as mess men. Whatever job you were given, you were all part of the Wardroom team.

I was given the very unusual job of being the passageway leading hand. This took me away from daily work in the Wardroom. This pleased me as it took me away from the officers who I had really started to resent because of their snobbery and upper class attitude. I had to do a two day course on board with a P.O. Seaman who was to be my direct boss and I was to be in charge of two teams of four. Our job was to clean and Glift and Gleam every deck from four deck and above. The only problem was that it was all night work. When we were in any ports we would have to go back to our own departments, but it was different and if anyone, including senior rates, didn't obey our instructions, they were put on defaulters table. We felt quite powerful really.

At the beginning of February we sailed from Plymouth on our way to America. Just outside Plymouth, the helicopter squadrons joined us from Culdrose in Cornwall. When we had gotten further out to sea the proper aeroplanes flew on, although we did have an aeroplane that joined us from Culdrose which was a plane with a propeller. I was told it was a Cod and would be our mail plane. Suddenly the ship was very busy and we were kept on our toes. People didn't realise what we were doing and we had to take lots of names.

After three months of doing night work I got quite fed up with it and went to ask my Divisional Officer if I could have a job back in the Wardroom. He said that he had a leading steward who also wanted a job change. If I went and saw him before doing the night shift he would have an answer for me. This I did and he said that I could certainly go back to the Wardroom. The replacement Killick worked in the air snack bar, but the boss said he really wanted me to work in the Wardroom bar. He said that I shouldn't do the passageways that night, but I was to report to the bar first thing in the morning.

I reported to the Petty Officer of the bar the next morning at 0800 sharp. I already knew the other guys and there was a leading steward who would work opposite me day on, day off. Four stewards worked two in each shift and another leading steward who did the paperwork would be required to help in the bar at busy times. The P.O. apparently couldn't do the paperwork, so he would help out in the bar when we needed a lift. He was a nice bloke, but I soon learned that he and the bookwork guy had words with each other every morning. The P.O. would then take bottles out of the cupboard and disappear with them. Sometimes there would be a couple of trips from the bar with a bottle. Also one of the Chief Stewards would come in every morning and have a double whisky. I got used to this strange goings on and followed the P.O. one day only to see him going into the Chief Petty Officers mess with a bottle and come out empty handed.

As time went on the P.O. changed to another P.O. and the paperwork killick was also given a job change. The new P.O. told me that he couldn't do the paperwork either, and asked me if I could do it. I had a look at it and found it was no different than we had learnt in training, so I agreed that I would do it for him. However, I made it clear to him that I wouldn't put up with any fiddles and that it would all be done by the book.

In the first two days I realised that by buying brandy, gin and whisky by the gallon jar and transferring it over to bottles there was a fair amount left over in each jar. When we were either alongside a port or when there was no flying on, the officers drank an awful lot of those items.

Some days we would go through about four gallons of each and would make up several extra bottles. Most of the time I would add it to the stock and hide it if we had a stock take. I told the Wardroom mess manager roughly what was happening to make it clear that I wasn't fiddling. He told me not to worry and that he would sort it out. Two days later a Lt. Cdr. came into the bar, said to me that he was a computer expert and told me he would feed some information into his computer to work out our bar stocks. That same day he came to me really full of himself and said that, from then on, there would not be any fiddles in the bar as it would be impossible to fiddle anything. It looked really good and I was quite impressed.

That night was a fairly quiet night in the bar, so when I went to do the books the next morning, I thought that we would be straight on. What I actually found was that we were half a bottle of brandy, half a bottle of gin and a few glasses of whisky up. When the officer came to see what had happened I showed him our ups. He was fuming and said that it was impossible since he'd proved it on the computer. He told me that he thought me, the P.O. and all the staff must be on the fiddle. I was so angry that I went straight to the mess manager and told him what was said. He came back to the bar with me and called the officer outside.

After a few minutes they came back to the bar and the boss said that, from then on, the P.O. would do the books and the Chief would teach him how to do it. I was to go back

115

onto shifts in the bar. I was duty that day and I, along with the lads, worked diligently to make it work properly. We were pretty busy as there was no flying. First thing in the morning, on a scrap of paper, I worked out the overs or unders in the bar. I didn't tell the Chief or P.O. but we were up on a lot of the usual.

After they had done the paperwork, the Chief asked me if anything had happened that night. He had us bottling up the booze that was over and told the officer that we were up a bit, but not a lot.

The officer then said, "See? I knew we couldn't go up each night."

After he had gone, the Chief said to me, "You know there are going to be a lot of different things up every night so, without getting yourselves into trouble, help yourselves to whatever you want whenever you are on duty. However, occasionally I may ask for something for my mess or the P.O. may want something for his mess."

Until that day I had never had brandy. My opposite number had not drunk it either and he told me that it was supposed to be okay with Cola. When I went on the next morning he looked rough. He said that he had drunk so much brandy and cola that he didn't think he would be able to keep up with it for too long. That night I didn't dare drink any and we had quite a busy night. The next morning the P.O. asked why I'd not drunk anything the previous night and I told him I was being cautious. He opened the spare cupboard and it had four full bottles in it. He told me that he and the Chief would take them away, but to make sure we kept it down.

Our biggest problem was that every time we got into port, we would have a cocktail party, usually in the hangar. So much booze was taken up to the hangar. Jugs and jugs of the main three drinks had to be made up and bars set up with those and other drinks on. There were few guests that left a cock and arse party sober. There also weren't many officers sober either. Most stewards wore their cocktail stockings. They were tropical long socks that were put on under bell bottoms. Each leg contained one bottle of spirits which would go to the stewards' mess for our own party or for starters before going ashore. The seaman and airman that did the washing up were always well oiled as well. Because the officers that didn't go ashore afterwards really got steamed, the bar ups were astronomical the morning after.

We visited a number of Naval bases in the United States, but the most memorable one to me was Mayport Virginia. It was a big Naval base a few miles from Virginia Beach. The American chefs invited the cooks and stewards to their open day on July the 4th (Independence Day) and I suppose there must have been seventy odd of us that went. They were so friendly and gave us a load of tickets for beer each. Two other killicks and I teamed up with a couple of these chefs that didn't have their wives and families with them.

We just sat on the grass drinking beer and eating hotdogs and burgers, all of which were free.

At about 1600 one of our mates had disappeared, so we went to look for him and saw that he was laid out on the grass, fast asleep. We tried to wake him but he got quite stormy with us. We relieved him of his beer tokens and went back to drinking. At around 2100 the bars had run out of beer so our host, that is the one who was left, suggested we go to the bars on Virginia Beach. We got Naval transport to the beach and headed towards Patrick's bar, which was covered in lit up shamrocks and pictures of little Irish fellas. As soon as we got in I put on an Irish accent, the bar staff loved it and were feeding us beers. I then stopped people coming into the bar and told them if they weren't Irish, they couldn't go in unless they bought us a drink. They all loved it, as did we. This went on until the remaining host withdrew and informed us he was going back to the camp.

After a while we decided enough was enough and we would go somewhere else. We left Patrick's and crossed the road towards another pub. As we were halfway across, a voice boomed out from outside the bar. It was a motorcycle policeman who called us over to him. As we got to him he told us we had been jay walking and he wanted our I.D.cards. My mate gave him his card, but I refused stating that we were not allowed to give our I.D. cards to anyone. He then called for a car to back him up and to take two prisoners.

I then said, "Do what you want, we are going."

Jan said, "Don't be stupid, Mick, stay here."

I started to walk away until I heard the policeman's gun click, and he said, "If you don't come back, I will shoot you."

I quickly walked back and stood next to Jan just as a police car pulled up beside us. We were pushed into the car and handcuffed together.

It wasn't very long at all before we arrived at the police station. We were uncuffed and told we were being charged with jay walking and being drunk. We were shoved into a cell which had at least twenty more people in it. In the corner we noticed a white lump laid out on one of the benches. It was our mate who had fallen asleep earlier. We sat chatting to him for a bit and he didn't know what had happened to him. We had several American flags on us, so I went over to the cell doors and was waving them about.

A man came up to me and said, "What are you in for, man?"

I replied that I thought we were in for jay walking.

"Man", he said, "That's serious in this state."

I asked what he was there for and he said, "I just shot my girl this afternoon, but I guess I will be out before you."

I then decided to shout at the police that they were all pigs and to let me out as I was a British serviceman. When I realised they were taking no notice, I decided to set light to their flags. I had a cigarette lighter in my pocket, took it out and started to burn the flags. One of them came over to me to ask what I was doing. I told him I was burning the flags. He tried to stop me but Jan stopped him and said, "He's just airing his feelings of how you Yanks are treating us people who are supposed to be your friends." The guy just walked away mumbling.

A little while later we saw the Naval patrol arrive and realised that we would be taken back to the ship. The cell door was opened up and we were ushered out. One of the policeman said, "Okay, you're free to go, but you must go straight back to your ship where they will sort you out."

It wasn't until we got outside that we realised one of the patrol was one of the leading stewards. When we got near the ship he said, "Out you go, lads. Give us a few minutes to get back to the ship, then you can either follow or go somewhere else." We decided that we would go back on board and say nothing.

Our next adventure was when we went to Jacksonville. Three of us decided to get away from Naval people and have a proper look at America. We hitchhiked out of the area and hadn't got very far when a big Cadillac pulled up next to us. The driver said that he was going to a drag racing event if we fancied it. We thought that it would be different. He was drinking a can of beer and offered us a can. We all accepted. We were going miles and all the time he and we were swigging beer.

We arrived at the drag racing track and it had been going for hours before we got there. Our driver, who was apparently a Chief in the U.S. Navy, wished us luck and bade us farewell. He had met some guys he knew and off they went for more beer. We realised that we had been forgotten by him, so we went to watch some drag car racing. It was very different for all of us, and we could get a beer and watch. We bumped into our driver a couple of times but he ignored us. After an hour it had all finished and everyone started to leave. We didn't have a clue where we were and had to find our way back to the ship. Firstly we went out of the site and got on the side of the road where we could start to hitchhike. No one was stopping, who would seeing three drunken British sailors in the middle of nowhere? So we walked and walked, mile after mile. We gave up trying to hitchhike and resigned ourselves to the fact we'd have to walk all the way.

As we started what seemed to be our tenth mile, a truck stopped near us. We didn't know if he'd stopped for us so we strolled up to where he had parked. He shouted out from the cab, "Hey you guys, do you want a ride back to your ship or what? Come on, get in."

We piled in onto the long seat and explained what we were doing. We all fell asleep on the journey, but woke up when we were going along a track. He said, "Okay, sleeping beauties, before we take you back to your ship, I thought you guys may like a drink or two in my home."

We arrived in this place which was just wooden huts and, all around us, were some people wandering round in Indian clothes while some were in cowboy type clothes. The driver then said, "You've guessed it, guys, you are now on an Indian reservation. Yes sir, we are all Cherokee Indians, stick with me and you will keep your scalps." Luckily he laughed then.

He invited us into his hut. There must have been ten other people in there, women, men and children. They all were watching us very keenly but none of them spoke. Our host gave us all a can each. We opened them up and the beer was very cold. We were asked if we would prefer a root beer, which our host was drinking. We all refused his offer and stuck with beer. Even the kids were drinking beer and we found that rather strange.

After a few beers a man came into the hut carrying a guitar. He asked, "Can any of you Brits play this thing?"

Paul said he could play a bit if it was in tune. The man threw the guitar over to him. Paul started to pick the strings, then said it would have to be tuned and started to tune each string.

After a few minutes the man said, "It don't matter if it's not tuned, we will all sing and none of us is Elvis, just play it."

Paul then started strumming it and began singing an Elvis song. Everyone in the room started singing with him; I've got to say it sounded worse than a shower of cats. Still, they all enjoyed it and asked to play some more. Paul started the same chords again but was singing a different song and once more they all joined in. After that song our host said, thankfully, "Right, I will give you a song then I will have to get these young guys back to their ship."

We all thought, 'thank God for that', and we all sang with gusto to another Elvis song. Then we left and they were all very friendly with goodbyes.

Trev had invited them all round to the ship the next day, it was to placate them, he'd said. We got back to the ship at about 0200 and were thankful to be there. Over breakfast the next morning, we were trying to work out how we were going to sort out our next day's visitors. We decided we would keep a low profile and stay away from the upper deck to basically ignore them.

We saw them arrive on the jetty in a few old cars. They were just waiting and waiting. Eventually our host from the previous night went up the gangway and asked the gangway staff where he could get hold of his friends John, Mike and Trev. He was told they didn't know of anyone with those names. He went back and told the others and they drove off, looking over all the sailors they came across. Needless to say we didn't go ashore the rest of the time we were there. However, some other sailors had invited our host and his wife and daughter on board a few days later. I passed them in one of the passageways, but to my relief they didn't recognise me.

After quite an eventful visit to two or three American ports we then sailed back to the UK and had a refit in Devonport. We had a couple of weeks leave, then I had to go back to HMS Pembroke to do my Petty Officers course. I really enjoyed the course and our instructor was a Manchunian guy. He was a really good bloke who was a bit of a big head. There were three leading WRNS on the course who were good fun and joined in with all the runs ashore we had. I don't think any of them paired off with any of the guys, but they drank as good and heavy. I remember one of them told us she was a white witch. Some of the others were taken in by this but I have never been a believer in the cults etc. Still, we had a laugh for a few weeks and, at the end of it, I passed with flying colours and also qualified professionally for Catering Officer.

We then had to report back to our ships. When I first reported for duty at the Wardroom bar I was told that I was to be made Leading Hand of the mess and my day time job would be in the Wardroom, in charge of the stewards doing the dogs work; cleaning the room and pantry, cleaning all the tables, the cutlery, the glasses and the like. I was still working under a P.O. steward but he let me do most of the organising. My team and myself had to ensure the dining room stayed immaculate as we were going to host the Queen, the Queen Mother, Duke of Edinburgh and the

Prince and Princess when we got back to the UK for the Royal Review in Torbay. That was something to look forward to, but first we were off to the Mediterranean for a few months.

Our first port of call was to be Gibraltar. I volunteered to be one of the ship's drivers before we left Guzz (Plymouth), so I had to take a driving test in Devonport dockyard and round the streets of Plymouth. This was done in a Land Rover and, although different to anything else I had driven, it was fun.

Chapter Six

RNAS Yeovilton, West Taunton Scout Group

My Daughter was born prematurely on the 4th November 1970 and I was on leave until the 2nd November. My Wife was in hospital, so I had to ring the Wardroom at HMS Heron and tell the Divisional Officer what had happened. He told me that if I could get along to Yeovilton as soon as possible to get a request form in for compassionate leave, he would then sign it and get it sanctioned. I got there within about half an hour, then I had all sorts of difficulties getting into the camp. I had never been there before so I was trying to get in the air station. The Wardroom gate was on the opposite side of the road and eventually I was guided there.

When I finally met my new Divisional Officer he seemed pleased to see me. He insisted that I meet the Chief Steward and someone was sent to find him. In the meantime I filled in a request for compassionate leave.

"Just put down for one week's leave", the Div. Officer said. "Right, when I sign that, take it over to the Regulating Office where they will sanction it and start you off on your joining routine."

Luckily the Chief Steward arrived just in time and said to the officer, "He doesn't have to do that, Sir, he needs to get home." He then shook my hand, welcomed me, and said, "Bugger off home, young man, I will sort everything else for you."

I thanked him and drove home as quickly as I could. That visit wasted about two hours of the time I should have been with my wife. I went to see my wife as soon as I could get into the hospital. She didn't look in a good way and I was worried as she had already lost a baby when we were at Portland. Anyway, as I said, my first child was born on the 4th November, she was only 3lbs 13 oz. and was tiny. She was in an incubator in the premature baby ward. We went to see her and she looked so small, especially with tubes and equipment all over her. She was given the last rights and was not expected to survive. We called her Deana as we both liked Dean Martin.

I joined Heron a week later on the 9th November. My daughter was still in the incubator so I made sure that I told my new Chief Steward all about it. He told me just to do my joining routine, getting my joining card stamped in loads of different places. He said that once I'd done that, I could go home. "I will put you on special duties until your wife and daughter are okay. You will have to come in each day, do a couple of little jobs for me and then go home. You can go when that's finished and I will see you at 0800 in the morning."

One of the young stewards was told to take me round the camp and showed me where I had to go. He was quite young, about seventeen I think, he said his name was Dave Sampson and he lived in Bridgewater.

So it was, I thought I must have died and gone to heaven as I had never been treated so well since I'd joined the Navy. I vowed to get my head in shape and prove that I could be a good Petty Officer Steward, I had passed my course in June that year, and I had qualified for a Catering Officer as well. I hadn't tried that hard to be honest, my intention was to leave as soon as I could. At that point, with the way I had been treated, I was having second thoughts.

Pleasingly for my wife and I, Deana was recovering well and I was enjoying life again. I eventually had to go back to normal duties and my first proper job was to become the Leading Hand of the Wardroom dining room. I worked under a Scottish Petty Officer called Dave Bremner, and I loved working with him since he worked so hard himself. Every day my team of stewards would have to clean the tables with vinegar and water, polish every glass, polish the entire silver cutlery and generally get the room ready for lunch. Before lunch we had to get all the cold meats out, get the carving board and knives ready, then sharpen the knives. We would also have to get the salads out, which two of the stewards had prepared. We had to keep the tea and coffee filled up and made sure there were enough cups and saucers out all the time. We made sure that the dirties were taken away and put into the dishwasher.

There were stewards all over the place, with some working in the pot wash who also had to make the salads. There were a number of stewards working in the officers' cabins, making beds and keeping the cabins clean. There were stewards who worked in the bar, in offices around the Wardroom, some who had to make coffee and take them with biscuits to different sites around the camp. There were also stewards who worked in the air crew refreshment bar, in the Admiral's houses, plus the Captain's house staff. Altogether there must have been 150 stewards.

Some of the men were squadron stewards who were at Yeovilton until the squadron officers embarked on ships. Some of the cooks and stewards lived in different messes around the camp, but they preferred as many as possible to live off the camp as there wasn't really enough accommodation for everybody. As long as you lived within forty miles they would give us a home to duties petrol allowance. This is what I did, and life was good.

We were in three shifts altogether. The bar staff and the house staff were different but we worked duty for 24 hours, then were off from midday the following day. Afterwards we were standby, where you would finish after doing any jobs the duty Petty officer wanted you to do, which could be anywhere from 1400 to 1600. However, if there was a cocktail party or a mess dinner on, you all had to work until they were finished. They didn't occur often, but were always on a Friday or Saturday. Each shift had a

Petty Officer Steward, two leading stewards and as many stewards that were available. Young Dave Sampson was in my shift and, if we were off or standby, I would take him home. It was quite a way out of my way but I liked young Dave and sometimes we would call into a little pub in Aller on our way home.

I also started my Taunton scouting in 1971. I was still in the Deep Sea Scouts but I was looking for a Taunton group to sponsor me. I looked around and went to a number of different groups, some cub packs and some scout groups. Because I was still in the Deepies we had the occasional meeting in Yeovilton. There were about twenty of us at these meetings and they were quite a laugh, and a lot of stories were told of meetings in different countries. Most of the really good stories were told of scout groups in the Far East. I'd had some history of some of these same groups, so a lot of comparing took place and many a funny tale was told.

Another strange thing that happened to me whilst at Heron was my promotion to Petty Officer Steward. It was particularly good because I had only received my first stripe (four years good conduct or four years undetected crime). However, I knew that once I was promoted I would be sent back to sea. I didn't mind that for myself but I was concerned about my wife.

My boss sent for me one day and asked, "How would you and your wife like to go to Bermuda for two and a half years, working for the Admiral?"

I was quite excited, apart from working for an Admiral, which I really didn't want to do since I was still not keen on officers, especially working so close with them. I told the boss that I would ask the wife what she thought as it was a big move for her and my daughter, and she would also have to leave my mother-in-law. We spoke about it and decided that I wouldn't want to go, what with my dislike for officers and having to spend a fair amount of time with him and his family, and the fact my wife really didn't want to go. I was due to leave in January 1974 anyway so I wouldn't finish the time needed for the draft. I told the boss a couple of days later. He was quite disappointed as he had recommended me for the job. A few days later I received a draft chit to join HMS Phoebe on the 3rd June 1972. I was to join her in (guess where...) Bermuda. We were going to be the West Indies guard ship. Although my wife wasn't particularly happy, I was over the moon.

Chapter Seven

HMS Phoebe, Great Ships Don't Come Round
Too Often

I flew out to Bermuda on the 3rd June 1972. I had to go via
Washington DC so it was quite an experience for me and I

had eight hours to kill. I put my bags in the property office and walked out of the airport. I then got a taxi to the White House. I bought myself a real American hot dog and sat on a bench just looking around me. That was the first and last proper hot dog I would ever have, it was revolting.

I was just about to throw it in the bin and a guy stopped me and said, "Please don't throw that away, I would love it", so I gave it to him.

Then a policeman walked up to me and said, "What are you, English or something? You know you shouldn't give to these hobos."

I told him that I was English and that I was sorry, I didn't realise it was against the law. He then told me it wasn't against the law, but that it wasn't to be encouraged. He showed me a good place to go for a meal, so that's what I did. After I had eaten a lovely steak and fries, I decided I had best go back to the airport, I realise now it was because I felt so vulnerable. All in all I didn't see a lot of Washington.

I then flew on to Bermuda. At the airport I was picked up by a Land Rover with a sailor driving it. He pointed out some points of interest on our journey to the Naval base. When we came into view of the ship tied up alongside I realised that was going to be my new home with new adventures to come. The mooring wall was full of paintings of ships' crests and was really quite impressive. As we passed the Admiral's house, I had to ask him what it was

133

like coming out here on draft. He said that it was fantastic; he also told me that a new P.O. Steward had joined a couple of weeks ago, and he and his wife and kids were neighbours of his. He said they all loved it.

When we parked alongside the Phoebe I did notice that it was immaculate and there were sailors over the side painting it, all they had on were blue shorts and sandals. They had music blaring and they all seemed to be enjoying it. The guys on the gangway were dressed in white fronts, white shorts, blue long socks and black shoes. As I got out of the Land Rover one of the gangway blokes came running down the gangway towards me.

"Are you P.O. Steward Screech?" he said.

"Yes", I replied.

"I'll help you get your stuff down to the forward P.O.s mess, my boss is the gunnery P.O. Doug Harris, he's also the bar manager the P.O.s mess and he told me to give you a hand."

When I got up the gangway to the ship and did the usual salute, I noticed a board which had every P.O. and C.P.O.s name on it. "Blimey", I said, "My name's on the board already."

"Yes it is, in case you want to go ashore this afternoon."

As I was being led to the mess, everyone that passed me asked if I was okay. This seemed to be such a happy ship, that I could see already. The bosun's mate rang a doorbell to the mess and it was opened by the bar manager, Doug Harris. He welcomed me on board and led me into what was the bar area, as well as the sleeping area. He introduced me to the P.O.s that were there, they all shook my hand, and one of them was a large man called Angel. Angel said that he was the mess president. He asked me if I wanted a pint. He told me that I was allowed four pints of beer a day and three spirits. He also told me not to worry about it as Doug would be able to sort it out in the secondary books. I said that I would love a pint of Red Barrel.

I was sat in the mess, chatting away, when the doorbell rang. "Is P.O. Screech there?" came a voice over the tannoy.

Doug went to the door and I heard him say, "Yes, alright Swain, I'll get him for you." He opened the curtain that led into the bar area and indicated for me to come to the door.

This little, fat, old looking man stood there and said, "You are supposed to report to me when you join the ship to do your joining routine. I am the ship's coxswain, you can call me Swain, P.O. Screech." He gave me a card and said, "You can probably do it all in your mess. Every day whilst we are in harbour is a half day for everyone, but it may be different for you as you are going to be the Captain's Petty Officer

135

Steward. Anyway, welcome aboard and you can bring that card back to me in the morning."

I managed to say, "Thank you", but he was gone. He disappeared into a room just down the passageway. I went back to the bar area and, when I got back, everyone was laughing at me.

"So you have met our make believe Master-at-Arms, then. We all call him egg on legs, actually."

I gave a strange look, but a guy called Ginge Monegram said, "He's called that because every time he walks he farts, and it stinks, you'll see."

That afternoon we had a few pints and, every time the door opened, someone else was introduced to me. They would then sit down and have a few drinks too. The person I was taking over from was called Joe. He was very well known in the steward's branch. He was a scouser and very funny. He wasn't going to leave the ship for a few days, so we would have plenty of time to get the handover done. Joe then suggested we go to the after P.O.s mess and he introduced me to some other P.O.s to grab a drink off them.

We went into the after mess and, just like our mess, the people in there were all having a few drinks. I was introduced to the other P.O. steward, Kenny Fitch, a guy who seemed to be alright, except he was talking to me as if I was one of his men. We then went up to one of the two

Chiefs' messes. We were invited in and given yet another pint.

Joe then said, "Let's go to get some dinner, then get back to the mess for a couple more pints. Don't worry about your allowance because I have been saving mine for a while."

The bunk I had been allocated was the middle one, back of the seat. It was facing the bar and my locker was around the back of the mess. I thought I would be getting Joe's bunk when he left, which was around the back where my locker was, and was in fact on top of the lockers.

I asked Joe about it and he said, "Sorry mate, but that has been allocated to one of the more senior guys in the mess, in fact he is in the bunk above you at the moment." He also said, "When you're at sea you can just put your bunk up, as not many people drink at sea so no one will take any notice. In fact, you will probably be better off staying there as the one over the lockers gets noisy at times and they always need a light on."

The next morning Joe got me up, told me he was going down to breakfast and that he would be up for me at about 0745. He would then introduce me to the Captain and the Supply Officer, our Divisional Officer. I put my white shirt and shorts on and, being a senior rate, I wore white long socks and white shoes. I went and had my breakfast and sat next to Joe. He waited until I'd finished, then took me up to introduce me to the Skipper.

On the way up he said, "You will really like the skipper but, whenever we are in port, he will disappear after breakfast and have a wander round the ship, then he will go ashore and meet up with his bit of stuff. She just flies to wherever we go, it makes our life easy. We have also got a leading steward to find work for, so you will have a lovely couple of months."

When we arrived at the Captain's cabin we went to his pantry first, where the leading steward was just waiting for the skipper to finish his breakfast. He went into the Captain's cabin and informed him that I was there.

"Send him in quickly, leading steward, and then send the Chief R.S. in to see me. If you could then lay out my beige trousers and the other bits that go with them, then I will be off." The Captain shook my hand and welcomed me on board before telling me that I wouldn't have a lot to do when we were in harbour. He said "I expect the P.O. steward has explained that to you. I won't be on board for the next two or three days. I wonder, when I'm away, if you would clean the gold on my old hat, P.O?"

I waited to speak to the leading steward to find out how everything went normally and for him to show me around the cabin to tell me anything I should know about the Captain and his habits. The Captain finished talking to those he needed to, then went and changed. He shouted for the leading steward to tell him he was off and he would be back in three days. With that, he was gone.

The leading steward told me his name was Dutchy Hollander before he showed me around the cabin and all the bits and pieces the skipper had for dinner parties and the like. He showed me the Captain's uniforms and they all looked in spotless order.

Dutchy said, "I always do the valeting for the skipper if you don't mind, P.O."

"No", I replied, "I don't mind at all, in fact that will really make me happy, but what is this about his cap that needs cleaning?"

"To be honest, I don't know how to clean that and I've been putting it off."

"Try and find me a piece of stale bread please, Dutchy", I said.

Dutchy went down to the galley to find some stale bread and brought it to me. I showed Dutchy how they taught us in training to do it. Unfortunately, it was so bad it didn't work. I asked Dutchy if there was any silver dip around, so I decided to clean this old hat with silver dip. It worked, but then I had to rinse it off with warm water. Although the gold braid was nice and clean the rest of the peak was a mess. I assured Dutchy it would be fine, but we would need to find somewhere else to dry it. Dutchy looked worried and, to be honest, so was I. We then left and Dutchy locked the Captain's cabin and pantry, giving me the spare set of keys. Dutchy said he was going ashore but he would be back at the cabin at 0800 in the morning. Joe told him we would be back sometime in the morning. I had never had a job before that I could go in whatever time I liked.

I asked Joe if that would be okay and he said, "Don't worry about Dutchy, he will just get on with whatever he wants to do."

Joe and I went to the P.O.s mess and had a pint of Watneys Red Barrel. Joe explained that the beer was a lot stronger than you would get in a pub as it was duty free and it had to be made stronger to allow for the sea conditions, etc. After a second pint Joe told me we had to go to the two Chiefs' messes and meet some important people. First we went to the after P.O.s mess where I was introduced to the two P.O. Chefs, the P.O. Caterer and all sorts of people. They all insisted I had a pint on them. By the time we left the P.O.s mess I knew I'd had a few drinks. Still Joe said we had to go up to the Chiefs' mess to meet the Chief, Jack Dusty, who was our divisional Chief.

Chief Dusty bought us a pint each, then the Master At Arms bought us one each. The Chief Shipwright, Mick, then asked me if I would like to taste this sauce he had bought ashore. I declined at first but he kept insisting that I try it. I told him that if he had a spoonful, then I would have a go.

140

Mick took a spoonful and put it in his mouth, so I had a spoonful as agreed. God, it was the hottest thing I had ever tasted. I had to rush out of the mess as quickly as I could, Mick followed closely behind and led me into the bathroom where we both washed our mouths out with cold water. Mick kept apologising between swigs of water. It was apparently the hottest spice in the world, and I never want to try it again. After this, we went back to the Forward P.O s mess. I met nearly all the P.O.s that day and we all sat around the mess drinking. Eventually I got into my bunk and slept until 0800 the next morning.

I made my way up to the Captain's cabin, saw that the pantry door was open and Dutchy was pressing the Captain's white uniforms.

"Morning Dutchy", I said.

He replied with a "Morning." He then said, "I'm a bit worried about the Captain's cap though, Mick, as the peak doesn't seem to have recovered." I had a look at it and, sure enough, the cap looked really sad. "Don't worry, Dutchy, I'll tell the Captain that it was my fault and offer to buy him another."

For the next two days I laid in my bunk until someone came in to open the bar, then I would get up, have a shower, get into my civvies and join whoever was at the bar. By 1200 the bar was full. I would go and have some lunch, go back to the bar, then go to the top of the hatch above the steward's mess and shout down to see if Dutchy was in. He would come to the bottom of the hatch, look up, see it was me, and shout up, "Everything is fine, Mick, the skipper will be back for lunch the day after tomorrow." That meant back on the piss for me, and to see if anyone wanted to go ashore. When I asked the people in the mess about going, they all said that Bermuda was too expensive.

That afternoon the Chief stores accountant came to our mess to speak to me. I invited him in for a pint, for which he needed little persuasion. He told me that P.O. Dusty who was stationed there wanted to take him and me ashore, particularly to the turtle sanctuary. Apparently he knew me from Osprey. The Chief (Screwy) then said he would appreciate it if I would go, and to make the excuse that he wasn't very well. I didn't mind as it was nice to get out of the mess. At 1400 I had a phone call from Screwy to say that Smudge was on the jetty waiting for me. When I got down on the jetty, sure enough, I recognised Smudge.

We shook hands and he said he was sorry that Screwy couldn't come, although it would have been a bit of a squeeze in his car. When we got there I could see why, it was a little Golf and already in there were his wife, who was a fairly large girl, and two boys of about four and six. The little car was rather cramped, but luckily his wife got in the back with the boys.

We first went to see an old wooden ship which was a copy of a large sail boat, it wasn't in water but stuck in cement.

Still, it had a crowd of people looking round it. Smudge then said, "We haven't got time to queue up, get round and get to the turtle sanctuary." So we got back in the car and headed straight for the sanctuary. This was all very man made and people were holding fishing lines over the pond so the turtles were grabbing hold of whatever was tempting them. A sign said that if you landed one you could keep it. Of course, no one caught one as they would just hang on until their fronts were out then drop off. Quite honestly it was boring and I couldn't wait to get back to the mess.

We arrived back just in time for dinner. I enjoyed the meal very much. That evening we also had a sing song in the mess. I was introduced to Angel Elliot who was a big guy and he had an American lady with him. He told me that he was a wrestler when he wasn't the ship's electrician. He said the lady was his fiancée and that he was going back to live in her house in Bermuda which was apparently huge. She had brought a pink telephone for the mess with her, which she said would brighten the place up. We couldn't refuse the phone as Angel was the president of the mess and what he said went. Mind you, he had a lot of mickey taken out of him behind his back. Doug Harris, the Gunnery Petty Officer, told me not to take too much notice of Angel as he was engaged to a policewoman in London, so he was full of shit.

We sailed from Bermuda after the ship had been painted (again). We were not going too far as, because we were the

143

West Indian guard ship, we would call into different ports even for just a day. The Captain would be taken ashore in a boat to meet local dignitaries, and then we would be off again. The most memorable for me was St Vincent. I went ashore with the caterer to see the ship's chandler and see if we could get any fresh food and milk. On the jetty, as we went ashore, we noticed a lot of men just standing there, looking after tons of bananas, apparently waiting for ships to come in and load them up.

After we had seen the chandler we decided to have a walk around the town while we waited for the chandler to be able to tell us what we could get from him. It wasn't much of a town, but there was a large football stadium...well, it was large for West Indian stadiums. As we got to the stadium we saw that the big gates were open, so we looked inside. The pitch was full of cows, sheep and goats all having a good old feed of the grass. Of course that meant that the pitch was full of animal droppings. There were two local men putting pitch lines on ready for the game against our ship the next day. I had put my name down to play the next day, but thought better of it.

We decided not to tell anyone when we got back to the ship as they would think I was just trying to get picked. Instead, when we got back, I went to see the club swinger to tell him not to pick me as I wouldn't be available.

"That's saved me a problem" he said.

That afternoon Angel was called to the flight deck. He soon came back to the mess with two men and a woman. One of the men was obviously local, while the other man and the woman were quite obviously British. As normal they were made very welcome, and we served them drinks from the reserve stock. The husband was a Welshman from Cardiff and his wife was from Bridgwater in Somerset. Someone asked them if they played darts, and offered to let them into the back sleeping mess where we played darts every day. His name was Dave and he was really a good dart player who looked a bit like Tom Jones. He won most of the games he played.

When they decided to go home they were quite pissed. They told us that we would be welcome to their local beach the next day which had a revolving bar. After that they invited as many of us who wanted to go back to their house for supper, beer and darts. We told them we had to go and watch the football match at 1030 and asked them how we would get to the beach. They told us that several of them were going to the match too, so when it had finished they would take us there.

The next morning the whole ship, apart from the duty watch, had been given the day off so that we could all watch the match. Nearly all the ship's company made their way to the football stadium. As we got to the gates the animals were being ushered out of the ground. Following behind them were a couple of dozen women sweeping the pitch with bamboo brushes and picking up the animal

145

droppings. They finished that at 1020 and both teams were invited to go on to the pitch. Our players still complained about the pitch being so bad and it still had quite a lot of droppings on it. At kick off they were still moaning, then the locals kicked off and scored straight away. The ship's team realised that if they didn't start playing as usual they would lose. The St Vincent players were individually good but very greedy and didn't pass to each other very much and so, despite the state of the pitch, the Phoebe players were so much better and ended up winning 10-1.

Outside there were several cars parked up to take, not just our mess, but any of the ship's company who wanted to go to the beach. It was a lovely beach and, sure enough, there was a large, revolving bar on it. We all settled down for the afternoon with swimming, sunbathing and drinking, it was a great afternoon. Then about at 1700 Dave came round to our mess members and started to organise cars to take us to his house. When we got there it was lovely, big and stood on stilts. There were ten of us and ten others, some were Brits, some locals, and it was properly organised. The supper was really nice and it was a very close darts match. Alice, his wife, then said she was going to ring her brother in Bridgwater, so she would ask him to ring anyone's family back home for us. She asked him to ring my wife in Taunton, but he couldn't get through. We had a very good night and arranged for several of their friends to come on board for a few drinks the next day.

The next morning I was called to the Wardroom, I was going to be running it for a while as Ken had got his Chiefs rank and had been told to work for the Captain until we got back to the U.K. There, Ken would be relieved by another Petty Officer. One of our stewards and one of the cooks had got into trouble at the revolving beach bar and were locked up in the local police station. I had to go with a policeman to court with the two of them. The police station was in the middle of nowhere but was next door to the courtroom.

The lads were brought into a room where I could chat with them. They were wearing some old clothes that the police had lent them and complained that they didn't have any underwear. It appeared that they had met two young girls at the beach and they had been skinny dipping among the rocks. The girls had left the sea before them, ran back to where they had been sitting and stole their clothes. The police inspector then came into the room and said they were going to let the boys go back to the ship, but they would like me to go to court to cross examine the girls who had been caught. The police took the boys back to the ship and I was guided to the court.

I've got to say I had never seen anything so funny in all my life. I had to sit on a bench with several people and just wait until I was called. The first case was a woman was in the dock for tripping a man over. The man went into court, where he was called by his Christian name. He went in on a crutch, swore to tell the truth etc, then swung the crutch round to try and hit the lady in the dock. The policeman in the court grabbed him and sat him down. The judge asked the lady how she pleaded to the charge. She replied that she was guilty. The judge bound her over to keep the peace and fined the man $10. The woman sitting next to me told me they were married and were forever in court. All the witnesses were laughing.

Next in court were the two young ladies who stood together in the dock. They were charged with stealing clothes from two English sailors. They were asked if they were guilty or not guilty, they both said "not guilty." The judge then pointed to me and asked if I'd like to question the two girls. I asked the girls what they had been doing on the beach that day. They both replied at the same time "skinny dipping" and, at that, the people in the court were laughing and slapping their thighs, I felt quite silly for asking the question.

The judge then said, "Guilty, two days in cells each".

At that the police inspector came, tapped me on the shoulder and said, "For your safety, you had better come with me back to the ship."

As I left the court several people gave me dirty looks and tried to trip me over. The policeman ushered me into his Jeep quickly, put his foot down and sped me back to the ship. When I got back, everyone in the mess was drinking so I naturally joined them and told them the tale of the court. It turned out a few of the lads had been attacked by locals, so everyone stayed on the ship that night. We had the local darts team over for our last game before sailing.

The trip back to Plymouth was uneventful. I was working a day on, half a day off with Dutchy. It was one of the easiest jobs I had done. The Captain spent most of the time either on the bridge or asleep in his cabin. When he ate, you could guarantee that there were a line of people waiting outside his cabin to speak to him. This made it quite difficult to serve him his three courses since people lingered in his doorway as he was eating and we had to wait until they were out of our way.

When we got alongside at Plymouth, several of the local mess members had their wives and families on board, so the mess was full of people again. The bar was open, so we were all back to drinking our allowance. Several new people had joined in Plymouth. Ken, the Wardroom P.O./C.P.O, was leaving the ship and going to Manadon, the training establishment for Engineer Officers. His relief was a P.O. Steward called Nobby Clark, a midlands guy who turned out to be a great singer and all round life of the party type of guy. There were no new guys in our mess though, which was a bit of a relief really.

Two days later we were off to Chatham for a small refit and to get some leave in for everyone. Once again we had a mess full of guests when we arrived at Chatham. Some of the families lived there as we were a Chatham based ship.

The first person I was introduced to was Angel's girlfriend, who was a City of London policewoman. Angel introduced her as his fiancée, so that was his second fiancée I had met within a month. He told me to keep my mouth shut about his Bermuda fiancée. Angel was leaving the ship a couple of weeks later as he was going out on pension. His relief came on board to see him as well and it turned out he would be a Chief by the time he joined but, because he was drafted as a Petty Officer, he would have to live in our mess. Most of us could see that would cause problems, and that was how it turned out to be.

Altogether on the ship there were a few changes of personnel, not least the Captain. I let Dutchy go on leave whist I looked after the new Captain. The new guy was a really super bloke, and I hit it off with him immediately. Also he lived in Taunton so I could see things going to my advantage. He had only been on board a couple of days when he told me he would be going on leave to Taunton for a few days, so it might be good if I took my leave at the same time. Of course, when we got to the station, it turned out he was going first class. We arrived at Taunton and his wife was waiting for him so the Captain asked me if I would like a lift home. On the way he asked me if I would be bringing my car back to Chatham in about three weeks' time. I said that I'd intended to and he asked if I could take him back. I told him I only had a mini, but it would be a pleasure. So it was arranged that I would pick him up at

0800 on the day. He then informed the ship that I was going to arrive late back that day as I was taking him back.

For my leave period my mother-in-law had arranged it that I could have a few hours work with Hatchers Removals whilst I was on leave. I thought that was money for old rope and I thoroughly enjoyed it. One morning, the Hatchers undertakers asked the boss if he could spare me to help him with a body. The boss said it was okay if I didn't mind. Off I went next door and there were two bodies being laid out, so I watched this with a great deal of morbid interest. I suppose I spent over an hour in there and I felt quite the expert when I returned to the storeroom to do my proper job. The boss told me to go home as we had nothing to do for the rest of the day, he told me not to worry as he would put me down for full pay, so I was gone.

After my leave it was great not to have to leave home at 0400 as I normally would have done. I found the skipper's house quicker than I thought I would, and waited a few houses down the road for the clock to reach 0800. Five minutes before he came outside with his wife, so I went straight up to his house. He and his wife kissed goodbye and she waved to me. The Captain only had a small bag which he slung on the back seat and climbed in beside me, he was a very short man, so it was no problem. All the way to Chatham he called me P.O. and I called him Sir.

When we were near Chatham, he said to me, "Would you like to park in the Captain's billet whilst we are in Chatham, P.O?"

I replied that I wouldn't mind.

He then asked me, "Is there any chance I could drive your car now and then, if I paid for your insurance, made sure I paid for maintenance and ensured it was always filled up with petrol, how does that sound?"

I said, "That sounds pretty good to me, Sir, but what about weekends etc?"

He replied that I could go home in my car every weekend, and if I could take him occasionally then that would be good. He then asked me, "Instead of sailing with the ship, whist in UK waters, how would you feel if you simply came to our ports in your car, and you let me drive it while we were in these ports?"

I immediately agreed. When we arrived at the ship I parked where it said, 'Captain F4 only'. The officer on the quarter deck was shouting for me to move as he was new and didn't know the Captain.

A dockyardie came to the car and said, "You're going to have to move, son."

The Captain got out of the car and said, "Is there something wrong? I am Captain F4."

At about the same time someone had pointed out to the Officer of the Day that the Captain was in the car. When we walked up the gangway, they all saluted the Captain and he made his way to his cabin. The Officer of the Day stopped me and asked what was going on and who I was. I told him that I was the Captain's P.O. Steward and that the Captain had told me to park there. He then said that apparently I was late back off leave and the supply officer and the coxswain needed to see me as soon as I was back, so I decided that I would call on the supply officer before I went anywhere else.

As I entered the officers' flat the supply officer, the coxswain and the First Lt were all talking to the Captain. I walked to the Captain's pantry and Dutchy was there.

"Where the hell have you been P.O? The whole world and his sea daddy are looking for you?"

I told him it was a long story, but I would explain it to him when I got my uniform on. As I turned to walk down the ladder the coxswain said to me, "Shit, Screechy, you're a lucky boy."

I told him I would explain everything to him once I had got changed. I carried on to the mess to get into my uniform. Of course all the people that were in the mess having a coffee break were interested to find out where I had been. As I was getting into my uniform I explained as I went along. I left the mess to go to the Captain's cabin and all

153

along people were asking me questions. I eventually got to the Captain's pantry, Dutchy made me a cup of tea, then stood in the pantry with his arms folded and said, "Well?" so I went on to explain to him what happened.

I then went on to explain to Dutchy that I didn't like his attitude towards me, standing there with his arms folded and more or less demanding to know what I was up to. I reminded him that I was his boss and that he was a rank below me. I then told him that if he wanted to remain as the Captain's leading steward he had better just do as he was told and keep schtum. Instead of replying to me he just stormed off and headed towards the supply officer's cabin.

In the meantime the Captain rang his bell, so I went into his cabin to see if I could do something for him. He asked me what was going on with the leading steward as he'd heard me telling him off.

I told the Captain what had happened, he nodded his head, and said, "You are quite right, P.O, I will get the supply officer to have a few words with him."

I explained that the leading steward had made his way to the supply officer's cabin.

The Captain then shot up from his chair, went to his door and shouted, "Supply officer to my cabin now, and bring Leading Steward Hollander with you."

I could hear the two rushing up to the Captain's cabin. In fact, they got to the door before I had even got to it. I excused myself as I went out and made my way to the pantry. I could hear the Captain speaking to them but he was fairly quite at first, then suddenly I heard him shouting at Dutchy and telling him that he was to work for me or go and work in the Wardroom.

He then said, "Supply Officer, give the leading steward until lunchtime to decide what he wants to do."

I then saw Dutchy going down the ladder. The supply officer remained in the Captain's cabin for a while longer. He then came to the pantry and told me to go into the Captain's cabin. Very unusually, as I went into his cabin, he invited me to take a seat.

The Captain then started by telling me what he had told Dutchy, and the supply officer sat and nodded at everything the Captain said. The Captain then said he wanted to explain to me how my job was going to be for the near future.

He said, "You will remain as the Captain's P.O. Steward at least whilst we are around the British Isles, but that won't be your only job. If it's alright with you, you will drive me home to Taunton each weekend we are in Chatham, and bring me back on a Monday morning about the same time as today. However, occasionally, I won't be coming back until the Tuesday and you will be the same. When we go to

Scotland I would like you to drive up to Scotland and join the ship, wherever it may be. I will then take over your car and go on some visits I have planned. The same applies when we go to Plymouth and Torquay and back to Chatham."

The supply officer then asked about when we were at sea and what I was to do then.

The Captain replied, "He will stay at home and allow enough time to meet the ship, wherever it may be. The leading steward, whoever that may be, will look after me at sea and he will have all the time off when we are in harbour, or whatever the P.O. wants him to do. I will pay for all the insurance on the car, and all the expenses such as petrol. How does that sound P.O.?"

I replied that I was very happy as long as everyone else was. The meeting was over and the supply officer followed me to the pantry.

"What do you think then, Michael?" he asked.

I told him that it sounded great, and asked if he would make any arrangements that had to be made on the ship. He assured me he would and advised that he'd need receipts for any of my expenses. Dutchy had come up before lunch and busied himself with getting the table ready for lunch and preparing the pantry. When he had finished doing that, he then apologised to me.

I replied, "It's fine, Dutchy."

He then said, "P.O, would you mind calling me leading steward or leading hand from now on, because you are my boss and I don't want to be your friend?"

I then said, "That's fair enough, I shan't forget that's what you asked. You serve the Captain's lunch and I will come and speak to you afterwards."

After the Captain had eaten his lunch, Dutchy was cleaning up the pantry and I asked him to go out to the upper deck for a chat. He sauntered out to the upper deck and stood looking at me.

"Look, Dutchy", I said.

"Leading steward", he replied.

"Okay, leading steward, just listen to what I have to tell you and don't interfere until I have finished. The Captain has asked me to leave you to look after him whilst at sea in British waters, while I am to follow the ship in my private car and arrive at any location the ship goes into. The Captain will then take my car and go wherever he wants to go. At those times, he does not require either of us to be in attendance to him. However, he will occasionally return to the ship with his laundry requirements etc. Being as you are his valet, you will be the one to carry out those duties."

I could see that Dutchy was getting really wound up with what I'd told him. He said nothing, but turned on his heels and went off in the direction of the supply officer's cabin. After a little laugh to myself I thought I had better wait in the Captain's pantry for either the supply officer or Dutchy to come and chat with me. To be honest, I was rather looking forward to it.

An hour and a half later, both of them came to find me. I've got to say Dutchy was looking quite ill at this stage and the supply officer kept putting his eyes in the air. "Can we go to my cabin, P.O? I think we need to explain a few things to the leading steward."

When we got there, the supply officer started the proceedings by saying to me, "When you told the leading steward what was going to happen with yourself and the Captain, you didn't mean that the leading steward would be doing all of the Captain's valeting, did you?"

I replied, "Well, yes Sir, that is what the Captain told me."

"Well", he said, "You will help the leading steward with the valeting duties, won't you, P.O?"

I replied, "Actually, Sir, I won't. I will, on occasion, help to clean the cabin when I return to the ship. However, if it is going to cause problems, Sir, perhaps I had better tell the Captain that I had better not do it as it is going to cause problems between Dutchy and myself, I'm sure the Captain will understand, Sir."

158

At that I got up, walked out of the supply officer's cabin and started towards the Captain's cabin. The supply officer chased after me and shouted, "P.O, I don't think we have finished yet."

I replied, "The thing is, Sir, unless Leading Steward Hollander is happy with it, I know there are two leading stewards who would love to do it, so I suggest that is what we do and Hollander goes to the Wardroom."

"Okay, okay P.O, I will sort something out, just don't tell the Captain."

I couldn't wait to get down to the mess and tell all my mess mates what had happened since they were all quite envious of my new role, and most didn't like Dutchy either, so it was a great feeling.

My next job was to work out the dates I would be at sea or at home. I then had to work out what I wanted to do when I became a civilian in a few months, and this new role would help me to prepare. The ship was sailing to Glasgow the following day and they were going to have a two week exercise first. That meant that I had two weeks of free leave. That evening I packed my civilian clothing and dirty washing, threw it all in the car and drove home. I'm sure my wife thought I had deserted when I got home that evening and told her I was home for two weeks. However, if things changed such as the ship going to sea for longer, or if it broke down, I would have to go back earlier. It still sounded like a good deal to me.

After two weeks leave I drove to Glasgow. I arrived there just in time to see the ship coming alongside. Some cones were put up on the jetty to indicate the Captain's car and the registration number of my car. I parked in that spot and made my way up the Gangway. The Officer of the Day was waiting for me when I boarded the ship. He told me the Captain wanted to see me straight away. I left my bags with the quartermaster and walked to the Captain's cabin.

Dutchy was waiting for me at the entrance to the Captain's flat (passageway). "Hang on a minute, P.O, I will just check to see if the Captain is available yet."

You can imagine what was going through my mind at that moment. I decided I would knock on the Captain's door and walk in, which is what I did.

The Captain was standing there in civilian clothes. "Hello P.O, how was your journey?"

Dutchy was behind the Captain putting out ornaments and had obviously not told the Captain I was there.

I then said to the Captain, "My journey was good, Sir. I thought the leading steward was going to tell you I was here."

Dutchy then said stupidly, "Oh, I forgot, Sir."

I gave the Captain the car keys and briefed him about the fuel, oil etc. He told the snake steward that he wanted a little private conversation with me. Dutchy left the room but I could sense him outside next to the door listening.

The Captain said, "The leading steward has not done a bad job, but I am asking the supply officer to think about him going back to the Wardroom." He winked at me, then told me that he would be gone for three days. He said he would be back for two days, and then he would be off for a further two days. Finally, he told me that the ship would be going to Plymouth, so asked if I would take the car home in four days' time, then leave it there until we returned to Plymouth. Another few days off, dear, oh dear.

I went into the pantry next and Dutchy was cleaning the silver. "Right, Leading Steward Hollander, I was wondering why you didn't tell the Captain I was here, and then why were you standing outside, listening to what the Captain was saying to me."

Dutchy replied, "I forgot to tell him you were there, but I didn't hear anything else, P.O, honest."

"That's fine then, you will be glad to know that I will look after the old man for the next three days, and then I will let you do the last two days in harbour before I drive off to Plymouth."

Dutchy then let it slip and said, "When will I be going to the Wardroom, then?"

I replied, "I didn't realise the Captain had told you that, I'll ask him what he means when he has dinner tonight."

"No, no", he said, "I accidently heard him tell you."

"Piss off, Dutchy, I don't want to see your face for three days, do you understand? Just get out of my sight, you're a liar."

When he had gone, I gave the cabin a quick once over and locked it up for three days. Over the next three days, I bumped into Dutchy once or twice around the ship, but he tried to avoid me as much as he could and we didn't say a word to each other. A number of other ship's company did ask me at different times why Dutchy was going to work in the Wardroom and why he didn't know the skipper wasn't on board.

The Captain arrived back on board at lunchtime on the day he said he would. I told Dutchy that I would sort the skipper out, but asked if he would come back to give him tea and his evening meal. Dutchy thought all his holidays had come at once, so much so that he started to call me Mick again and told me how sorry he was about his attitude. I told him that he was forgiven.

He then asked, "Do I have to go back to work in the Wardroom? I would rather stay here."

I told him that I would check with the skipper. That teatime I went to see the Captain and asked him if Dutchy would be staying where he was. The Captain told me that it was up to me, but he did do a good valeting job.

"Anyway", the Captain said, "Sit down, P.O, as I need to have a chat with you about what's coming up."

I sat down just as Dutchy brought the Captain's afternoon tea in to the cabin. "Could you bring the P.O. some tea and cake, leading steward, I think you owe him that much, don't you? After you have done that you can have the rest of today off as I won't be here tonight and the P.O. will clear up."

During the next few days a number of new crew joined the ship, including the new Captain, new Master at Arms to relieve the coxswain, and a new P.O. steward to relieve Kenny Fitch. He was a fresh-faced guy who was the life and soul of the party. He was called Nobby Clark, a Midlander who was married, had two kids and lived in a married quarter near Chatham. He, like Ken, was my senior, in as much as the senior steward on the ship, but we were more or less the same age. He was to be in our mess and had one of the posher bunks at the back of the mess.

We carried out a lot of exercises over the next few days to make sure everyone knew their jobs and the new Captain was happy with everything. Of course, my job was to change, the Captain would not require my car anymore, so I was back to working with Dutchy. It's strange how things happen but Nobby really liked Dutchy, and over a couple of pints asked me if we could swap one of his leading stewards for Dutchy. I explained that Dutchy had been threatened with that a few times lately, so all in all I wouldn't mind.

The next morning Nobby was walking up the Captain's flat with his arm round Dutchy and, as they got to the pantry, Nobby was shaking his head. Dutchy went into the Captain's cabin and Nobby said, "I think he is rather strange, don't you? He wants to stay and work for the Skipper."

I replied that I thought it would be the case.

A few days later we sailed for Norway, which was quite unamazing except that Nobby entertained the locals with his singing. We had a really good night, but of course we got drunk and were threatened by a few Norwegian fishermen. We were only there for a couple of days and most of the things people went ashore for were pornographic stuff and vibrators which were for sale on street corners out of machines. However, the beer was very expensive and not that great either.

We were then off to Lubeck in West Germany, where we were going to go along a River to Lubeck Army Tank Corp training camp. All the V.I.Ps, senior civil servants and senior German officers came to visit the Captain and others but, when all had gone, Doug, who was now mess president, had an invitation for all Chiefs and Petty Officers. We could attend the officers tank training grounds, where we would be taken onto some tanks for the afternoon. After that we would be invited to attend a banquet at the junior officers' mess in the camp. To be honest, there was nowhere else to go, so several of us volunteered.

We were taken by German Army buses to the start-off point, where we were introduced to the men we would be riding with. The thing is, it was nothing that we would normally choose to do. However, we clambered into the tank we were allocated to. It was the most horrendous ride on or in anything most of us had ever ridden. The drivers were trying to find the tallest, longest, most uncomfortable hills we could have wished for, then we drove over vehicles and it made a few more sea sick than they had ever been at sea. We were all quite thankful when it had finished and we were led to the beer.

The tables were set out in a square shape and we were all invited to sit around the square, all trying to sit with one of the other Brits. I ended up on the far side of the table next to Alf and we had an officer cadet on each side of us. We drank all the beer they had in the mess, so they then had to go and borrow some more from another mess. When we were on the last lot of that, the Germans had decided it was time for us to go back on board. A German officer then stood up and told us the Germans would like to thank us all for coming, and they all stood and raised their glasses. Alf then turned to me and said that one of us should do something similar and, since I was in the middle

165

of the top table, he thought it should be me. I then got to my feet and raised a glass, saying, "We would like to thank you all, and up your bucket", at that everyone stood up and said, "Up your bucket."

The Captain waited until he was sure that Dutchy had gone, then he said to me, "I am going to tell you something that only a handful of people on the ship know. You must ensure that the only people you speak about it to are the First Lt, the supply officer, the Master at Arms and the P.O. Caterer. No one else must know until I tell the ship's company the day before we get into Plymouth. When we get there, work is going to start straight away on changing the name of the ship to HMS Hero, as we are going to be the star of a series on BBC called Warship. The BBC will be coming on board to take photographs of different parts of the ship and they will be making those departments into the studios. The week after we will be inundated with actors, make up and costume people."

He continued, "Whilst at sea they will have free reign to use the Wardroom, the Chiefs' messes and the P.O.s' messes. They will be able to buy drinks in these messes, but they will only have allowances as senior rates. In other words, four pints of beer a day in harbour and only two pints of beer at sea, while they will only be allowed three tots of spirit a day. You may be required to help the oncoming Wardroom P.O. Steward and the P.O.s' messes bar accountants. We will be going to Gibraltar for some filming, where the TV crews will join us again. I'm afraid you will be back to normal duties and take complete charge of my entertaining and day to day operations. Have you got an opinion on this lot, P.O?"

I replied, "I'm shocked, but pleasantly surprised and very happy, Sir."

"Enjoy your next few days at home and tell the Master that you will need a train warrant from Taunton to Plymouth, and we will see you there." To be honest I was dying to tell someone about what the Skipper had told me, but I did keep quiet.

After getting home a few days later, I naturally told my wife what was happening and that I would be leaving my car at home for a while. Going back to Plymouth on the train, I felt like life was more or less normal. As I was waiting for the ship to come alongside, though, there were delivery vehicles waiting on the dockside including food wagons, beer wagons, NAAFI board wagons, you name it, they were there. I don't think I have seen so many delivery wagons waiting in one go. It would mean that, when the gangways were down, every one of the junior rates on the ship would be storing supplies while all the senior rates would have to bring the barrels of beer on board. Meanwhile, the officers would be sitting in the Wardroom with their feet up drinking tea or coffee. When I was allowed on board, I got changed into number eights (working uniform) and went to join the chain of senior rates bringing the beer on board. After that, I went to ask the Captain if he needed anything, then Dutchy and I had a cup of coffee while he explained to me what was happening as the ship's company had been told the previous night.

The ship's company stood down (stopped work) for lunch and had to go back to it until 1700. It was then suppertime, and all the stores were on board apart from Alf and his number two and a few other volunteers finishing off stowing the remainder of the stores away.

Alf saw me and shouted, "I'll have a pint in half an hour."

It was more like an hour before he had completely finished, but we sat down in the mess and discussed with other mess members about the forthcoming BBC crew coming on board. A lot of attention was put on how we were going to account for the duty free booze they were entitled to, or not, as the case may be. We also spoke about how and when the ship would physically feed them all. The big problem for me was that I had been made the social secretary in the mess, which meant I had to arrange the mess entertainment both at sea and in port. We knew that we were going to Gibraltar, but no mess tried to arrange parties in Gib as none of the local girls, nor the service girls there, were interested in coming on board ships to have limited amounts of duty free booze, especially as the booze in Gibraltar was duty free anyway. The duty free we had was still limited to each individual. For that reason I thought I would not have to do anything in that way. I was sadly mistaken.

The next day there were several BBC crew on board taking photographs and moving things about, plus meetings with our Lords and Masters in the Wardroom. The stewards were run off their feet taking teas and coffees all over and, when lunchtime came, the officers were inviting BBC crew to have lunch and drinks. The chefs suddenly had to allow for a lot more people for food and, to put it mildly, they were pissed off. The stewards had to ensure there was enough cutlery and crockery available to relay the one Wardroom table several times. As you can imagine, they were also pissed off.

That night, as many of the ship's company as were allowed went ashore to get ready for what we believed would be a very tough period coming up. Most of the P.O.s went ashore with each other and generally we had a brilliant run. Some of us went to Ivor Dewdney's pasty shop outside St Levin's gate, or to the fish and chip shop, before going back on board. There, someone would be able to open the bar without the keys that had been returned to the duty officer. We all sat round with a pint and ate our nosh. We were all aware that, early the next day, we would all be busy and that would be the case for a while and, quite honestly, we were dreading it.

Chapter Eight

HMS Hero, Warship and the BBC

At exactly 0900, the BBC crews arrived in Royal Navy buses from HMS Drake. They came up the gangway one by one and some of them were carrying big bags. They all got together on the flight deck where they were briefed by one of their people and the First Lt. All the big bags they were carrying initially went to the Captain's flat. All the people from the BBC were told they could use any of the officers' or senior rates' messes and they were allowed to swap and change whenever they liked. This was going to cause pandemonium in itself since it meant they could all have an account in each of the messes, which would also cause problems with duty free allowances. If they were to use the officers' mess there were no restrictions, but in the senior rates' messes they were only entitled to what we were entitled to.

Within half an hour we had twenty BBC crew arriving in our mess. One was supposed to be the Admiral and he was called MacDonald Hobly. The Captain was Donald Burton, who was supposed to be Commander Mark Nialls and David Saville, who was supposed to be the First Lt, Lt. Cmdr. Beaumont. There were also cameramen, make up artists and wardrobe. Women were frowned upon by the Admiralty to go to sea. They were lovely people, one and

170

all, and they shook everyone's hand. Then David Saville asked if anyone would like a drink.

We all sat quietly until Doug spoke up, and he said, "I'm very sorry but we are only allowed four pints of beer each with three spirits and, I'm afraid, that includes all of you."

"Bollocks", replied David, "We have been told we're exempt from all that. Just pour out what people want and I'll take responsibility."

With that, all the people in the mess agreed to have a drink on this guy.

In the meantime, Jan left the mess and, on his way out, he said, "I'm going to sort this out."

Whilst he did this we all settled down to have as many beers as we were offered by the BBC crew. Each of them were given a mess number and handed a chit book to put in their orders. A few of them settled down in the mess while others went to the other messes and began lashing the members up in each of them.

Jan eventually came back with a big smile on his face. The BBC crew had all gone back on the Royal Navy buses to their hotels and I didn't see any sober ones leave the ship. Jan told us that he had been to meetings with the First Lt, the Master at Arms and the BBC representative to discuss the allowances. The supply officer was going to see the Admiral to find the official line. The Captain had said it was not for the ship to police the BBC, so Jan reckoned all was going to be well.

That night, all allowed ashore went ashore again and, once more, we had a really good night. We were aware, though, that we were going to sea at 0800 the next morning. We were only going until the early evening for some filming to be done at sea, and in and around the Wasp helicopter. The crew were going back to their hotel that night, most of them were going to fly to Gibraltar and a few were coming with us for some more filming at sea. I think it was the first time in my career that we went straight to Gibraltar, no exercise, no drills, rough through Bay of Biscay, but that's all part of the fun.

When we went alongside in Gibraltar, the BBC crew were waiting to get on board and they took up the entire gangway getting all their equipment on to the ship. The press were taking photos of HMS Hero while all sorts of hangers-on from the Admiral's staff and officers from HMS Rook also came on board. It was suddenly a very crowded ship.

Once the BBC crew had got all their equipment on board, they headed straight for the messes to have a pint. It was like having your oppos come aboard, it was great to see them and they were far more relaxed than before. The main actors spent most of their time in the officers' mess, in a way that said a lot about them. Don't get me wrong, they were all very nice people, but..!

After the BBC crew had gone to settle in their hotel, we all tried to give the mess and ship a good clean ready for the next hectic day. We had to make sure our uniforms were smart and clean, our caps were pristine with not to many bow waves in them, and that our shoes were gleaming. I was told that I was to spend the whole of the next day filming with the BBC and needed to have my raincoat ready to cover my badges.

When everything was ship-shape, Jan, Alf and I went ashore. We visited a few hostelries before we decided to have a look at Sugar's Bar which, as it implied, was run by a guy everyone knew as Sugar. We had a laugh in there, then got some fried chicken with chips and sauntered back on board.

When we were sat around the mess with a few other blokes, Jan said, "I know, we will put on a party for the BBC crew that use our mess, we could do it on Friday night so that none of us have to start too early on Saturday."

Someone said, "We can't have a party without girls, can we?"

Everyone agreed it wouldn't feel right with about thirty six blokes and a few drinks, so Jan, in his wisdom, said, "Mick Screech, as the social sec. it's down to you to organise the women."

"You're having a laugh, aren't you?" I replied, "When have any of you gone to Gibraltar and had a social? No women or girls are interested in all the bullshit of coming on board a Naval ship with all the problems to get enough spirits and things."

All those present looked at me and one or two said, "Come on, Screechy if anyone can, you can." So I agreed to try.

The next day, a few Petty Officers, Chief Petty Officers and I had to muster on the jetty, carrying our Burberrys over our left arms. It was so hot; I was praying that we wouldn't have to wear them. We were all told to follow the director around the other side of the dockyard where there would be a boat to take us out to this old rust bucket for filming. One of the P.O. Artificers was asked to go with one of the crew. He was taken out to the old rust bucket whilst the rest of us had to wait. We sat on anything we could that wasn't going to get any muck on our uniforms, and that's where we stayed for about an hour and a half.

Some of the senior rates were telling the BBC crew that if they were still there in ten minutes, they were going back to the ship. It was so hot and we hadn't been given a drink so we were all getting pissed off. A few minutes later, the boat came back with our Tiff mate. He told us that he'd had to put on his raincoat and go up and down the rope ladder onto the rust bucket. He'd had to do it so many times so they could cover up the fact that he was Naval, not customs. He then had to look as if he was searching and, when he came across this big locker, he had to open the door where, there before him, was a naked lady, supposedly dead.

He was so full of, "She was gorgeous, with dirty great big knockers." He said they only took two takes of that scene.

In the meantime, they had bought us all a drink and a sandwich, which was very pleasant. They then briefed us on what was going to happen next. They looked us all up and down and finally decided that they would only need four of us, so the rest could go back to the ship. That did cause a bit of consternation among those that had to go back.

We who were left were told we would need to put on our raincoats to cover over our badges. We would have to keep our heads down as much as possible to cover our cap badges. They would then be filming us getting on the boat, occasional filming of us going out to the rust bucket, filming us climbing up the rope ladder and also getting onto the rusty ship. There we would be again briefed of what was next. When we had done it and were ready for the briefing, we were told that two of us (the smallest) would be required to climb up the narrow ladder to the crow's nest and pretend we were searching it. It was only just big enough for us both to get in it. The other two had to pretend they were searching on the main deck.

Apparently we were being filmed from ashore and they would zoom in. After we had finished, we were told it was

175

now complete and we could go back to our ship. We were so glad that it was over, we were sweating and dirty. That late afternoon all the BBC crew had gone back to their hotel and the mess and ship were fairly quiet. Most of us were fairly tired so after a bit of cleaning and uniform pressing etc, we all sat down and had a pint to talk about our day.

Filming the next day was done mostly ashore, in the dockyard and the Admiral's offices and house, so we didn't see much of the crew again. Those of us that were involved with the filming were given the day off. Jan told me to get Alf to go ashore with me and find some women to come to our party on the Friday. We did as we were told and, everytime we saw any women, we gave them an invitation to come to the ship. They all declined, as we thought they would. We went back to the ship and Jan asked how we got on. We told him that, as expected, we got nobody.

"Right", Jan replied, "Tonight, after our scran, us three will go ashore and get the amount of women we need."

At about 1830 we three went ashore on our mission. We headed straight to Sugar's bar, how did I know that was going to happen? When we arrived there it was obvious that a party was going on and there were about twenty gay guys all around a table with a birthday cake and candles. They were all singing happy birthday to Gloria, who was stood partly dressed as a woman. When they had finished,

Jan went over to them all and wished Gloria a happy birthday.

Next, in his best gunner's voice, he shouted to them all, "How would you like to come to a party on a Naval ship? There will be booze, food, dancing and, above all, some lovely BBC people."

They all screamed and shouted and were delighted to come as they had never been invited on a Naval ship before. Jan told them about how things had to happen whilst on a ship, and asked if any of them would like to come dressed as women since we wouldn't mind.

The next day, when a lot of the BBC crew had come to the mess for a drink, Jan said, "Right, you lot, Mick has arranged for you to come to a party in the mess on Friday evening, he has arranged the female guests and we will all have a great time."

Every one of the BBC crew was quite excited. Some of the mess members were a bit shocked, but most were happy.

Several mess members came to me and asked on the quiet, "How did you manage that in Gib, Mick?"

I told them all it was thanks to Jan.

One mess member, who was a Chief, really sidled up to me and said, "You're full of shit, Screech, no one has ever arranged a party in Gib. If they turn out to be blokes, I'm going to smash your head in."

I told Jan of the threat afterwards, and he said to leave it to him.

For the next couple of days, the booze had to be sorted through difficult double paperwork and Alf had the food to sort while Nobby, the Wardroom P.O. Steward, had to sort out a punch bowl and some ingredients for a punch. Others had to make the mess look good. The batteries on the doorbell had to be fixed. Every time some women were about to come into the mess someone had to say at the doorbell and speaker, "Flag eight", and, at that, all members of the mess had to stand up to greet the women.

Friday night came and the BBC crew who were coming were all in the mess, it was more cramped even before our guests of honour arrived. The sailor at the gangway made an announcement over the ships tannoy, "P.O. Steward Screech, you have guests on the gangway."

I went to the gangway and there they were, twenty men dressed as women, the sailors in that vicinity were wolf whistling while comments were made. I had to sign them all onto the ship, then I led them to our mess.

At the door I pressed the bell and said through the speaker, "Flag eight", before opening the door.

Everyone made space for them on the bottom bunks. They were all given a glass of punch and introduced themselves around. A couple of the BBC crew were gay men and they were in their element, but most people seemed very happy. The Chief that had threatened me raised his fist to me. I just stood behind the bar all evening watching what was happening.

At about 2330 people started to leave the mess, some were going up to Sugar's bar and others were going back to the BBC crew's hotel while a few left with someone on their arm. Some didn't come back until the morning. Those of us that stayed cleaned the mess and had a last pint to discuss how the evening had gone, and the general feeling was that it was a great night. The next couple of days went by with constant filming on and around the ship while everything else was going on as normal. At the end of that filming we were heading to Lisbon for a couple of days, then onto Chatham where I was going to have my last days on the ship before going outside.

Lisbon was a typical Naval port, there was a street full of bars and prostitutes. Most of the mess were going to go ashore and have a few drinks. I was going to be treated by the lads as it would be my last foreign visit before leaving the Navy. One of the POs even offered to pay for a prostitute for me, although I won't mention any names, Pat. Of course I declined the offer, but good of him. Thanks Pat.

179

Because we were probably the oldest group of people sitting in the bar, we were inundated with girls coming to our table and offering us their bodies at different rates. To be honest, we were getting fed up with it and kept telling them to go away in short sharp jerks. Anyway, as I said, they were offering themselves from 40 escudos upwards. All except one lady, she appeared at the door of the bar in a long evening dress. She caught everyone's interest, especially one of our numbers, who sauntered to the door, took her arm and brought her over to our table. She was lovely looking. He told her to come and meet his friend. As she walked over to me I noticed she had St. Vitus' dance.

She stroked my hair and said, "Please come to have sex with me, I am very good and I will only charge you 10 escudos."

Pat then leant over the table and said, "That's the one, Mick, I said I would pay for one for you."

"Thanks, Pat", I said, "Can you let me have 20 escudos, to pay for the taxi as well?"

"Course I can", he replied and threw me over the money.

I got up, held the lady's arm and walked her over to the door. When we got there I put the 20 escudos into her hand, said, "Thank you very much", and showed her out of the door. I then walked back to the table, thanked Pat and sat down.

"You bastard, Screech, you owe me 20 escudos."

Everybody laughed and took the mickey out of Pat for the rest of the evening. It wasn't too bad for him though, I gave him half the money back.

The next morning we headed back to Chatham without incident. When we docked, the Watneys rep came to the mess.

I sat down next to him and said, "We could do with some Watneys tea towels in here, you know."

He wrote it down and asked if there was anything else we would like.

"Well", I said, "There are one or two things we could do with urgently, and two other things I would like personally. First of all, we would like twenty Watneys t-shirts and twenty Watneys jockey hats before my last run ashore on Thursday."

"I've got those in my car now, shall I get them?" he asked.

"No, have a pint first so I can tell you what else I need," I said. When he settled down with a drink, I asked, "What are the chances that I could get some duty free cans sent to my home address?"

He replied, "I'm sorry, Mick, but even I wouldn't be able to get that. I'll try but I think it's a no."

181

"Okay", I said, "But there is just one more thing, are there any vacancies at Watneys for reps jobs like yours?"

"I wouldn't be surprised, my boss is with me tomorrow so I will ask him."

You would never believe it but when I rang my wife the following night, she told me that a Watneys van had been to our house and dropped a case of beer off. "Did it say Duty Free Only on the case?"

"Yes", she replied.

What was even stranger was that evening, when the rep came on board and had someone with him. He asked for me by name, so I rushed to the gangway where the rep introduced me to his boss. We went to the mess and had a pint each.

"I hear you were asking about a job with us, Mick, is that right?"

"Well, yes, I did actually. Have you got anything?"

He then informed me that there was a job in Liverpool looking after ships that came in, including any warships. The pay was £12,000 a year plus commission, and there was a house going with it at Aintree. I thanked him very much, told him when I would be available, and accepted the job!

My last night on my favourite ship and all the mess members were buying me beer and rum. We all put on the Watneys baseball caps and the Watneys t-shirts that were sent to the ship and off we all went on a pub crawl of Chatham. We had such a laugh, and people laughed at us as well. But overall it was a great night, spent with great mates, from a great ship.

My next and last move was a couple of months at RNAS Yeovilton, then to HMS Drake to hand in my Identity card, gas mask and anything else they could get off me.

Chapter Nine

Civvy street, here we come

Needless to say I didn't take the job with Watneys, although I really fancied it, but the wife didn't want to up sticks and move to Liverpool. Instead I had to look for something to do in Taunton. For the first and last time in my life, I had to go to the Job centre.

When I got to front of the queue, I sat opposite this young fella in a suit. "And what sort of job are you after?" he said.

"I don't know really, I have been a steward in the Royal Navy, I have served a lot of royalty and have been a valet to Admirals and the like. I have had lots of experience with beers and wines, and accounting for them."

"So how would you feel about selling insurance, then?" he replied.

I told him I had never thought about it, but asked why he'd thought that would suit me.

"That's the job most servicemen do when they come out", he replied, so it was arranged that I would go for an interview at Refuge Insurance that afternoon.

I dressed in a suit and tie, and went into the Refuge Insurance Offices. They were very busy and I was pretty much ignored for about ten minutes.

Suddenly, a girl said, "Are you wanting to see someone, love?"

"I have come for an interview", I replied.

"Do you want to buy some insurance then, love?"

At that point a middle aged man came out of a room and said, "Mr. Screech, come in." I was a bit nervous as I hadn't had a job interview for years. "Right, sit down, Mr Screech, and relax."

He asked me what jobs I had done since leaving school, so I told him my works history. He asked me if I had ever been a boy scout, so I told him that I had and that I was still in the Scouts, although I didn't have a troop in Taunton yet.

"In that case you have a job at least, Mr. Screech, as you are just what we are looking for."

I told him that my name was Mick and that my dad was Mr. Screech. He thought that was funny, but still introduced himself as Mr. Rowan.

"If you could start on Monday, Mr. Screech, you will have to make your way to Tiverton where you will meet the rep from Exeter. He will show you around for the next couple of days, give you the paperwork and then leave you to it. We will then expect you here on Thursday at 10.00am."

I met the rep from Exeter as planned and, although he was not very friendly, he showed me the round for the week.

From the Friday onwards it was to be a different area. So far it was all fine, I just had to collect weekly or monthly insurance premiums. On the Thursday I was to pay the monies in and meet my colleagues. So far so good, but they weren't the type of people I was used to. When I had done everything I had to wait to see Mr. Rowan while everyone else had finished for the day.

Mr. Rowan invited me into his office, "You have done very well so far, Mr. Screech. Did the Exeter man tell you anything about selling some policies though?"

I told Mr. Rowan that he hadn't told me anything about selling policies, but that he had sold a couple himself and sent me ahead of him.

"Right", said my new boss, "On Monday I will come with you and we will sell some insurance so that you can make some income."

So that is what we did. It was a slightly different route on the Monday in that it was nearer home. Mr. Rowan was as good as his word and he sold three policies that day, but he put them all down on his name. I tried, but the rest of the week I didn't manage to sell any policies at all. When I did the paying in on Thursday, Mr. Rowan called me into his office again. He really gave me a hard time about not selling any policies. He told me I had better improve the next week or they would have to let me go. That day I went home and looked at the local paper for job vacancies.

Horlicks Dairy were advertising for a milkman. I thought it looked good, and was something I could handle. They gave me an appointment for the Friday afternoon. It was a great relief when I got there and they told me that the round I would have was the biggest in Taunton, and I would have a brand new walk-in float. I would be doing the Bridgewater Road to Creech St Michael round. They wanted me to start on the Monday week, at a suggested time of 0500. I went straight back to gave my notice at Refuge Insurance, who I had great pleasure in referring to as Refuse Insurance from then on.

I arrived at the dairy on the Monday morning at about 0430. There were already milk floats reversed up against the fridges, with milkmen and women loading up their floats.

An old man called Reg called me over and asked if I was Mick Screech, and I replied that I was. He told me that he had already lined my float up and my milk was behind it. He showed me how to load it up onto the float. Everyone was wishing me good luck.

He said, "Every morning you can come in at any time from 0330 and bring your float over here. I will give you your allocated milk and goodies, then you just have to load up and get on your way when you're ready. If I am too busy to get your stuff ready, just look at your list and help yourself. What you bring back is then credited to your account."

One of the other milkmen sidled up to me and said, "Try to get in about 0400 as Reg is too busy then, so you can load a few extra crates to your float. In your float you have a big cab as well, so you can get more in."

Reg then gave me a book with my round number on it and said that if I just worked through the book page by page, I would be fine. I started out from the dairy at about 0500 and ran up the paths and drives of my new customers. Since people are all different, some just left money in envelopes or wrapped in paper for the amount of milk they wanted, some had set orders for the week and some left little notes to say if they wanted orange juice or eggs, butter or bread etc. My float had room for loads of extras. We also sold Corona.

I didn't have much more than a crate unless someone had a regular order. In one place going into Creech there were five or six houses, all of which were my customers. They all had standing orders except one. She used to leave the money in a tin box for the amount of milk they wanted. There was milk on one side and Corona bottles the other side with money for that separate. I put her milk in, then saw what Corona she wanted and put that in as well. This went on for the rest of the week.

One day an upstairs window opened and a lady shouted out to me, "Milkman, can you please just leave me the milk I ask for, and not the Corona?"

"Sorry Mrs, but I didn't know you didn't want it from me, you just left a note asking for Corona and I gave it to you."

"Well, I don't leave a note out for the Corona man to leave me milk, so don't be so stupid. I don't want Corona from my milkman, do I?"

"Get a different box for each, then I wont get confused", I replied.

"Oh, just leave me two pints of milk today, you idiot, and ignore the Corona."

At that I took the milk out of the tin, put her money back and walked off. When I got back to the dairy that day, the boss asked me why I didn't leave the lady any milk. I told him what she'd said to me and he told me that if I didn't want to serve her milk, I didn't have to. Instead, every day, I just walked around her house.

She resorted to shouting out of the window for me to leave her milk, though I ignored her. She then thought her daughter would be able to change my mind, no way, and then her husband came out, stood up next to me and said, "Milk, now."

I replied, "Bog off. Until I get an apology, and a regular order of milk and Corona, there will be no more milk for you, you'll have to find another milkman."

On the Saturday, the lady was waiting for me. "I'm sorry", she said, "Can I now have two pints of milk? I have a pound's worth of sixpenny pieces you can have if you want."

I let her have two pints of milk and put in my book in front of her, 'two pints of milk every other day, two bottles of Corona a week, and paying cash every Saturday'. She was happy to agree to that.

On a few of the households, quite a lot of money had been owed for a long time and, at 4d a pint, I found it hard to get the owings off these people. One house had built up a bill of over a hundred pounds and the boss asked me if I could chase it up. I went back to this house in the afternoon and caught the owner there.

"I wonder if there is any chance of collecting what you owe?" I asked.

When I told the man how much it was he nearly fainted. "Look", he said, "I've got a big vat of cider round the back, if you bring however many bottles you have, I will fill them all up and you can sell the cider to your mates."

I went back to the dairy and told the boss what the customer had told me.

"Right", he said, "When you get round to his house tomorrow, you tell him that is a deal as long as he pays off the milk at two pounds a week. Any milk he has will have to be paid for as and when he has some, and tell him that we will bring a float full of bottles round tomorrow and fill them all up."

So the next day I ran through my round until I got to the cider man's house. I knocked on the door, and the old fella came out.

"Did you talk to your boss then, milkman?"

I told him what the boss had said and he agreed whole hearterdly, so I dashed back to the dairy as quick as I could. When I got there the boss was waiting with a float full of Corona bottles on the back, there must have been a hundred crates.

The boss said, "When you're ready, we will be on our way then, boy."

It was a motor float, the boss got into the driver seat and we were off back to the cider house. When we got there, the boss and the customer shook hands, then they went into the house for a cup of tea while I was filling up the bottles with cider. I had filled about thirty cases up when the vat was getting very low and the stuff coming out didn't look very nice.

The boss came out and said, "That will be enough, boy, let's just load the float and get out of here."

When we got back to the dairy there were about ten milkmen waiting for us. The boss was selling them four or five bottles of the scrumpy for two pound a bottle. He asked me how much I wanted and I said, "Just two, please."

"You can have them for nothing boy, for helping me."

When I got home I gave my next door neighbour a bottle and put the other one in the fridge.

The next morning, when I got to work, old Reg brought out my milk and goods. He said, "It's a bit strange, only you being here. I know two have rung in sick, but there's usually a fair few of you here at this time."

I loaded and went straight out to work. When I got back to the dairy, I was the only one there apart from the girls in the office. I asked them where everyone was, and one girl said, "Oh, we had six phone in sick, so the boss and old Reg have gone out with a couple of the others to do all the rounds."

I guessed what had happened there so just went home. My neighbour's wife said, "Bloody hell, Mike, Dave drank that cider you gave him and he has been in bed all day."

I didn't stay as a milkman very long after that. I looked for a job as a company rep. There was a job advertised in the local paper for a rep to sell mixing machines called Bamix. I applied and was given an interview at home. The guy was very nice, he showed me the machine and how good it was.

When he had finished he told me that I had the job and that, on the Monday week, he would pick me up in my company car. After that he'd take me to his home in Sherbourne where he would show me what I had to do. The following Monday I was to go to Sheffield and do a salesmans course, but in the meantime I had to practise the procedures to go through at a demonstration. I could also use the car whenever I wanted, which was an old, bright yellow Ford Escort.

The following week I started the salesmans course in Sheffield and, though there were about ten of us, only two of us were from Bamix. We were put up in a nice hotel, all got together in the bar that night and had a good time. On the Thursday we had to go out and knock on doors with our products to do our best to sell at the door. Ray, the other Bamix rep, and myself went together. On the first day of knocking and demonstrating we sold ten machines between us. When we phoned our boss that night he was really happy, but told us we wouldn't get any money for selling those as it was all taken into consideration. We would only get basic wages.

Ray was not happy. He left the course that night, leaving his Escort and all the gear he had, and went home. On the Friday the boss came up and collected Ray's stuff with the car. He waited for me to finish the course.

When we met up he said, "I'm so sorry, Mike, but you are going to have to go to Cornwall next week to carry out the demonstrations the Cornwall rep had organised."

I also had to arrange and pay for bed and breakfasts whilst in Cornwall and claim it back the next week. The first demonstration was to be in Lisguard at an old peoples' club. To set up these demonstrations took about an hour and a half. We were told never to stand on a stage, but to be at the same level as the potential customers. However, the organisor in Lisguard said "If you can't do it on the stage then don't bother as there will be so many people here, there won't be any room on the floor."

So I relunctantly set up on the stage which had two sockets, which was just enough. The people surged in at 1900 and I couldn't believe how many there was. I was introduced and strolled onto the stage, where everyone clapped me. One of the first demonstrations was mixing flour with water, it was supposed to settle and, when the bowl turned over, it would stay where it was. You were then supposed to get a member of the audience to hold it over their head to prove it. Because I was on the stage, I thought I would just hold it over my head. You've probably guessed it, it all poured out over me. The audience all burst out laughing, they obviously thought I was a comedian.

My last part of the demo was to grind coffee beans in a grinder that was part of the kit. When I plugged it in, nothing happened, so I found the other socket and plugged it in again. This time the grinder worked. I left it grinding, turned to the audience and explained the cost. Again, the audience burst out laughing and, as I looked around, I could see what they were laughing at; the grinder was on fire. That was the end of that.

As I was clearing away at the end, a lady came up to me and asked, "Are you a Londoner, son?"

I replied that I was.

She then said, "That's why they didn't like you, and your tattoos were showing. These Cornish people are a funny bunch. I'll tell you what though, I will buy one of those machines off you. Here is forty quid darling, okay?"

I had a couple more daytime demonstrations to do but, truthfully, my heart wasn't in it. I also had one more evening one to do. I went there in the late afternoon to have a look at it. There was a small hall which was in the middle of nowhere, with two bungalows just down the road. I told myself that I was not going to be bullied into working on the stage that evening. A note on the door said that the caretaker lived in the first bungalow, so I went to the front door and knocked. A lady answered the door and I explained that I was doing a Bamix foodmixer demonstration in the hall that evening, and asked her if I could possibly have the keys so I could set my things up.

"Oh no you're not, dear, you are doing it here, we have some people coming up from the village to watch. You're welcome to bring your stuff in and set up if you want." We got to the kitchen and she said, "There's the table, dear, is that big enough? There will be about eight women coming so they will just fit in here nicely."

"I'm sorry," I said, "Neither this room nor the table are big enough, perhaps we had better cancel."

"Well, we could go in the dining room, there's more room in there and a bigger table, but it's solid oak so I can't move it. If you wait for my husband to come he will help you to move where you want." So I agreed to wait.

Half an hour later, her husband came and asked me where I wanted the table. Between us, the man, his wife and I moved the table. The lady then set about getting enough chairs in there for the audience. Meanwhile, I set up all my kit, including new machines to sell. The husband came in with a cup of tea each and we sat down to enjoy. Whilst we were sitting with our tea, the husband started to ask me questions. I then thought I would ask him a very important question.

"Where are the plug sockets in this room?"

He replied, "We've got none of them 'ere, boy, this house be all gas. Your things don't need 'lectric, do they?"

There and then I knew my life would not be in selling. I was apologising and so were they. I left that bungalow, drove home and made my mind up. I was going to the recruiting office the following day and I was going back in the Navy!

Epilogue

Many people who read this will know that I have always had a good sense of humour and I have always had a laugh and enjoyed myself. During the times I have had in the last few years, it may seem that, sometimes, I have been pretty sad. To be fair, I have been. The thing that has got up my nose mostly is the bullies I have encountered over the years. What worries me a bit is that most of these bullies have not realised that is what they are.

I have encountered lots and lots of them, some of whom had positions of power in the forces and feel they have the right to be better than others. Some have been in scouting as well. These are sometimes the worst bullies. You do get the odd child that is a bully and, normally, they can be sorted. However, when some people become leaders, it is not enough to dictate to kids, they start to feel empowerment over the other adults. They don't know they are doing it most of the time. When they become District and County Commissioners they forget what scouting is all about, (again they don't realise that). In all my years of Scouting I can count on two hands those in power that stayed as nice and compassionate people.

All in all, my nine and a half years in the Navy weren't all bad. I met some really great and funny people, some of whom I'm pleased to say will be friends for life. I've also met some great people in scouting. I am still serving with the scout movement and have made some lifelong pals there, too.